Ten Things That Matter from Assessment to Grading

Tom Schimmer

Ten Things That Matter
from Assessment to Grading

PEARSON

PEARSON

Feedback on this publication can be sent to editorialfeedback@pearsoned.com.

Pearson Canada Inc.
26 Prince Andrew Place
Don Mills, ON M3C 2T8
Customer Service: 1-800-361-6128

ISBN: 978-0-13-272510-1

Vice-President, Publishing: Mark Cobham
Publisher: Bill Allan
Research and Communications Manager: Chris Allen
Managing Editor: Joanne Close
Project Editor: Lisa Dimson
Developmental Editor: Janice Dyer
Copy Editor: Kate Revington
Proofreader: Linda Szostak
Indexer: Noeline Bridge
Permissions Editor: Rachel Irwin
Production Coordinator: Jessica Hellen
Cover and Interior Design: David Cheung
Composition: David Cheung
Manufacturing Coordinator: Karen Alley

1 2 3 4 5 TCP 15 14 13 12 11
Printed and bound in Canada

Table of Contents

Chapter 9

Chapter 10

Acknowledgments

I am very proud of this book—it represents my first foray into educational writing; however, I am well aware that an occasion such as this doesn't happen to an individual like me without a huge amount of influence at work and support given. With that, I must thank several individuals and organizations for their contributions.

The staff and students of Vancouver College (1991–99): Vancouver College provided a professionally challenging, yet supportive environment within which to begin my teaching career. I have come to realize we were doing some fairly progressive stuff for the early 1990s. Vancouver College was a wonderful place to begin my career.

The staff, parents, and students of School District No. 67 (Okanagan Skaha): In particular, I acknowledge Summerland Middle School (1999–2003), McNicoll Park Middle School (2003–06), Princess Margaret Secondary School (2006–08), Penticton Secondary School (2008-09), and the district office (2009–11). I have learned and grown significantly in every place

I have worked in the district; I have also enjoyed the experience. School District No. 67 is an exceptional district that always puts students first!

Rick Stiggins, Steve Chappuis, Jan Chappuis, and Judy Arter (Assessment Training Institute): If not for ATI, I may not have developed as clear and as deep an understanding of the role that formative assessment can play in developing confident learners and in ensuring that students maximize their academic success. You are colleagues and friends, you have given me consistent support, and you have provided me with opportunities to present at ATI conferences. Thank you!

Ken O'Connor: Your mastery of sound grading practices is the benchmark for the rest of us to strive for. From you I have learned that teachers can grade in a *productive and accurate* way that is supportive of students, informative to parents, and rewarding for teachers. Over the last few years I have come to appreciate your support and encouragement. I am also happy to call you a friend and colleague.

Mark Cobham, vice-president, Publishing, and Joanne Close, managing editor of Professional Learning at Pearson Canada: As a new author contending with many rewards and stresses, I found it much easier to persevere knowing that you both strongly supported my efforts.

Lisa Dimson, project editor, and the rest of the editing team at Pearson Canada: You have helped present the ideas that drove this book in a way that will make sense to the reader. I am grateful that a dedicated team of professionals has focused on turning my manuscript into what, I trust, is a book that will have a positive impact on all those who read it. I greatly value your patience, support, and willingness to guide me.

Andrea DeVito, Cindy Russill, Lisa West, Steve DeVito, Darcy Mullin, Naryn Searcy, Myron Dueck, Ben Arcuri, and Chris Terris: Your generously given contributions have improved the book immensely and will serve as examples to other educators seeking to implement effective practices with their students. Beyond these contributions, I value our relationships, both personal and professional.

Bill Allan, publisher, Assessment, at Pearson Canada: Honestly, this book would not have happened without you. Thank you for seeing something in me that I didn't necessarily see in myself. It is because of you that I am a first-time author! Your unwavering belief in me and this book has meant more than I can express. I am also glad that our professional relationship has grown into a friendship.

And finally, my wife, Monica, and my children, Samantha and Adrian: Everything I do is dedicated to you and all that I am is the result of your love and encouragement. There is something extraordinary and inexplicable about a family where members accept and support one another unconditionally. You give my life much of its meaning!

Tom Schimmer
April 2011

The author and publisher gratefully acknowledge the contributions to this book made by the following reviewers:

David Hall *Curriculum Consultant, Prairie South School Division #210, SK*

David Manuel *Vice-Principal, Chilliwack School District, BC*

Ann Moore *Coordinator, Support & Evaluation South Shore Regional School Board, NS*

Anne Mulgrew *Educator (retired), Edmonton Public Schools, AB*

Paul Rose *Program Specialist, School Development and Assessment, Western School District 10, NL*

Lauren Wilson *Principal, Renfrew County DSB, ON*

Introduction

> *We know how to use classroom assessment to make success a driving force in the learning life of every student.*
> *We no longer need to accept the assessment legacy of our past. We know better.*
>
> **Rick Stiggins**

I believe that most teachers are focused on doing the best possible job for their students and are implementing the practices they feel will be most effective. However, some things we do inadvertently undermine student success and artificially make it harder for students to succeed and for us to accurately report their progress. During this book I will challenge some widely held beliefs about what students need and how they should be supported. Such direct and honest challenges are necessary if we are to shake off complacency and rethink how we do things.

We must also all be willing to try something new. In my family, no one is permitted to say they dislike a certain food until they have tasted it. When my son was very young, he would pick up a piece of broccoli and move it slowly toward his lips. Before the broccoli even touched his mouth, he was shaking his head, certain he wouldn't like it. While we knew the result was inevitable, we still *made* him try it—he has since become a relatively sophisticated eater. The premise of trying something rather than prematurely dismissing it holds true for educational ideas.

Looking for a Topic That Resonates

Ten Things That Matter from Assessment to Grading is intended to begin—or continue—the conversation about the priorities teachers should set when moving toward more relevant assessment and grading practices within their classrooms. It is not intended to be a collection or synthesis of the entire body of work on assessment, instruction, grading, and their impact on student self-efficacy. Rather, its purpose is to suggest the most important aspects of assessment for learning, sound grading practices, effective instruction, and positive relationships that teachers should focus on. A user-friendly guide, it also addresses *how* these ideas can be put into practice at the classroom or school level. All partners in the education system can use it.

Each chapter sets out to identify priorities, highlight big ideas, and inspire teachers to explore and implement the practices that will make the biggest positive difference for students. Chapter structure is outlined below:

1. A short preview outlines what the reader can expect from the chapter.

2. **Big Idea:** Here, the focus is on reviewing the current research behind each aspect that matters. The text summarizes the most important work on assessment, instruction, and grading.

3. **Putting It into Practice:** Most critical to the reader are the examples of how theory is put into practice. This section presents ways in which the research has been interpreted and implemented at the classroom, school, or district level.

4. **Tips for Communicating with Parents:** The existence of this feature emphasizes the need for clear communication with parents. Ways to work with parents in order to keep them well informed are outlined. Although brief, this feature is important.

5. **Guiding Questions for Individuals or Learning Teams:** This section provides questions for deeper exploration and discussion to further build fluency with the content and the capacity to implement with high fidelity.

6. **Suggested Readings for Further Study:** A list of a few recommended readings is provided for those wishing to explore each topic at more depth.

I hope that as a teacher, you will find a topic (or more) that resonates with you, prompting you to act, implement, explore, discuss, and debate both within yourself and with colleagues. Even where practices have already been implemented or explored, their outline here will serve as a quick reference or supplement to support deeper implementation. The ideas put forth are not presented in any sort of ranking. You can delve into any chapter of interest—there is no need to read chapters in a certain order.

Anticipating a Paradigm Shift

Let's assume that you have decided to establish some of the routines advocated in this book.

Anything that presents as being *different* needs to be explained to parents. The research available between the time they graduated from high school and when their children entered the system is significant. It isn't necessary to seek their permission for new routines; however, if we as teachers don't communicate ahead of time, we will likely have to return several phone calls, schedule some appointments, and answer a lot of email.

Most of our current parents expect their children to experience school in ways similar to what they did. Most had school *done* to them. If they were assigned zero for work not handed in, for example, many would be surprised if their children do not receive zero. If their teachers were tough, they want us to be tough too. This expectation is significantly higher if children attend the same school as their parents did, even more if they had the same teachers! Schools, however, are continually changing and evolving.

Especially as you establish new routines in the middle of the year, take the time to inform parents of *what* is changing and *why* you're changing it. Doing so keeps parents connected to their child's school experience. In the end, you will find that parents have the same reaction as their children. They will view the *new* ideas as more clear, transparent, learning centred, reasonable, fair, and thoughtful than the old ideas.

The thoughts within this book reflect the fundamental shifts of a new paradigm in education, one centred on assessment for learning and sound grading. This new paradigm, like any, won't come easy. As Richard Brodie (1996), the original author of *Microsoft Word*, suggests, a new paradigm goes through four stages before being accepted. First, people are complacent as a new idea is *marginalized* as off the wall, as not a serious threat to the status quo way of thinking. Second, complacency fades as the new idea persists. People then begin to *ridicule* it as inconsistent with what they believe to be true. Third, as the new idea gains acceptance in some circles, ridicule turns to *criticism* from those whose reputations were built on the previous way of thinking. Finally, when enough people make the leap to the new paradigm, it gains psychological and intellectual *acceptance.*

Brodie suggests that realization of these four stages—marginalization, ridicule, criticism, and acceptance—is inevitable. Over the past decade, each stage has presented itself to varying degrees in various places. So, if you work in a school where most of the staff are at one of the first three stages while you have accepted an idea, stay the course. Know that effective practices always emerge as new routines, even if that emergence takes a while.

Try one or more ideas in this book that are new to you. As Lao Tzu, the ancient Chinese philosopher, once said, *a journey of a thousand miles begins with a single step.* Find the courage to take that step. I know you will be surprised at how quickly the learning environment in your class improves, how positive your relationships with students become, and how your assessment, instructional, and grading repertoire expands.

Chapter 1

Being the Change Matters

You must be the change you want to see in the world.

Mahatma Gandhi

A tug-of-war is taking place in education. On the one hand, change is inevitable. On the other hand, change can be difficult and is often resisted.

Understanding the change process is important, not just from a step-by-step perspective, but from the perspective of being aware of how people respond emotionally to the prospect of change. Being open to potential areas of growth, while understanding the emotional journey, allows teachers to navigate their way through an education system that continues to evolve.

Innovative assessment and grading practices may not change the world, but they can and will significantly improve the experiences and success of the students in our schools. Although the prospect of change can be daunting, the time to act is now. The best educators are continually renewing, reflecting, and growing. Change presents new opportunities to learn professionally and to work more effectively with students. Never allowing themselves to settle professionally, effective educators seek new knowledge, understanding, and strategies to make the classroom experience the best it can be for their students.

Big Idea: Change Is Up to You

"Change is inevitable. Change is constant." These words by Benjamin Disraeli, a literary figure and British prime minister twice in the 1800s, could not be more relevant to our discussion of education. In many ways, today is the best time in history to be an educator. We understand more about student learning and achievement than we ever have. Whether it is new understanding of brain research, instructional practices that produce unparalleled results, or our ability to teach and support all students, including those with special needs, the potential effectiveness of our school system has never been greater. Trying to maintain some sanity while keeping up with the emerging body of research, however, can leave even the most seasoned teachers intimidated. The research on *best practice* often feels relentless and overwhelming. That said, change within our education system is going to happen whether we resist it or not.

It is important to set the context.

The focus of this book is not on *change for the sake of change*. Rather, the focus is on meaningful change for the purpose of professional growth and, ultimately, the success of our students. Change is often encouraged for the wrong reasons and, as a result, is doomed to fail from the beginning. Whether a colleague is completing a master's degree, an administrator wants to leave a legacy, or you want to establish yourself as a leader, implementing anything without a minimal level of research, planning, or support will have limited (if any) success and likely won't be sustainable. Others will be left feeling as though they've been tricked, that the implementation was self-indulgent, misguided, and unnecessary. This perception will have ramifications when the next *latest and greatest idea* comes along. We can't implement every suggested idea without confirming its validity. Meaningful change—change that we feel compelled to implement because of the empirically sound research and the potential benefit to our students—is our professional responsibility.

Challenged by Change

Change is something that, for the most part, happens to us.

The most obvious example of change in our society is technology. The rate at which the newest electronic devices become obsolete is staggering. While it might feel as though we've always had the Internet, only during the mid-1990s did the Internet become accessible and usable for the average person. When I began my teaching career in 1991, the Internet, while in existence, was not a tool I had access to. In fact, I didn't even know it existed. Our students, though, don't know a world without laptops, cell phones, text messaging, flat-screen TVs, GPS, Facebook, and Twitter. While all of these technologies are prominent now, that wasn't always the case; someone had an idea, people took action, and our lives were changed forever.

Technology evolves to address a need for improvement. When new technology falls short, corrections are made and new versions are released. When technology falls short, we don't say, *I knew cell phones wouldn't work or whoever thought a laptop computer was a good idea didn't have his head screwed on tight enough*. We wait for the next model.

The world's first commercial, hand-held cell phone, Motorola's DynaTAC 8000X, received approval from the U.S. Federal Communications Commission in early 1983. On March 6, 1983, the DynaTAC 8000X was made available for purchase. The idea of portable communication was revolutionary. Consumer demand for the phone was high, despite the hefty price tag of about $4,000 (in 1983 dollars)—waiting lists were in the thousands. The phone measured 33 centimetres (13 inches) long by 4.5 centimetres (1.75 inches) wide by 9 centimetres (3.5 inches) deep. The DynaTAC 8000X lasted eight hours between charges, provided 30 minutes of talk time, and took 10 hours to charge. The "brick" phone, as it is now sometimes referred to, changed personal communication forever.

Today, a cell phone measuring 33 centimetres (13 inches) long would be unmarketable. Cell phones are much smaller, more powerful, and far more diverse. The DynaTAC 8000X allowed no access to the Internet, no email, no text messaging, and no picture-taking capability.

Our ability to embrace new technology stands in contrast to our lack of desire to embrace the new "technology" of education in our profession. If we have no problem with the new features of our updated cell phones, why is it so difficult for some educators to embrace pedagogical advancements that could revolutionize our classrooms?

Putting It into Practice

If change is inevitable, why is it so hard to achieve? Teachers need to address this question.

It is human nature to resist change. In fact, it is a foible as human beings to stoutly defend an established position despite overwhelming evidence against it (Hawkins, 1995). People are creatures of habit who find comfort in their established daily routines. For many, these routines bring a sense of predictability to lives that can, even at the best of times, feel chaotic. While some industries thrive on progress and the latest advancements, education systems, despite the efforts of individual teachers, can be unusually slow at adopting and adapting to the new knowledge that emerges from the research.

Even if the situation is ideal, people still have a social-psychological fear of change (Fullan, 2001). This fear, coupled with a lack of technical know-how or skills to make the change work, makes it difficult for teachers or schools to move forward. Resistance to change is normal. In fact, Fullan suggests we should embrace those who resist change for two reasons:

1. Resistors sometimes have ideas that we might have missed. People's reasons for resisting change are valid to them. We need to respect them enough to hear their views as it is possible they have an idea we have never thought of.

2. Resistors are important to the politics of any implementation plan. Ignoring resistors will eventually take its toll on the planned implementation. Whether during or before, it is easy to sabotage any new direction if one is determined to do so.

The bottom line is that we need to understand that change, while inevitable, can be difficult for some people to embrace. Many of us have difficulty changing our morning routines, let alone changing important things such as not smoking, eating healthier, or exercising. Our habits bring us comfort, but they can also be our demise. As changes are proposed, it's important to remember to keep an open mind.

Keeping an Open Mind

One thing that has fascinated me over the course of my career is the mindset that develops within the teaching profession. This mindset has intrigued me so much I began to think about the things teachers say and how they would translate to other professions. Keeping an open mind implies not being stuck in a mindset where change is next to impossible. Below are four examples of quotations we would never hear in other professions, but that, unfortunately, are all too common within education.

"I've had this computer since 2000. Why would I change computers now?"

It would be inconceivable to hear this kind of proclamation from any other profession. Even teachers are more apt to embrace a change in technology versus a change in pedagogy. In Grade 11, I took Chemistry. My sister, 10 years my senior, had the same teacher for Chemistry. She described his methodical practice of keeping all of his lesson plans in manila envelopes and how he painstakingly pulled the plans out of the envelope for fear they might be damaged. My sister kept all of her high-school notebooks in our attic so, 10 years later, we were able to compare her Chemistry notebook with mine. What surprised me, even at 16 years of age, was that they were identical. My sister's notebook was much more tidy, colourful, and pristine (even after 10 years in the attic!)

than mine, but the content was identical. Now to my teacher's defence: Chemistry is, by and large, Chemistry, and just as the events of the Roman empire don't change in the 21st century, basic chemical laws are essentially fixed. However, even though I benefited from not having to take notes for the rest of the semester, I felt that the teacher had taken the easy way out.

"I'm too busy performing heart surgery to pay attention to the latest research techniques."

If your prospective surgeon said this, you would likely walk out of the surgeon's office, never to return. However, some teachers maintain a similarly cavalier attitude about research in education. Teachers are too busy to review several journals every month. It is our professional obligation, however, to keep ourselves current, much in the same way surgeons had better know what the latest research suggests about the surgeries they are going to perform. Making the time to stay current, either by choosing one educational journal to review or committing to one article per month, will help keep us aware of what's happening in our field. Education continues to evolve, and we have to keep up if our classrooms are going to remain relevant to the students we teach.

"I'm sorry, Kevin, your second driving test was excellent, but when I average it with your test from September, you still fail."

Reporting to parents, as we will discuss later, is arguably one of the most important things we do. How we construct the grades we report is equally important; otherwise, the grades become meaningless. This notion will get significant attention in Chapter 9 when we examine improvement. Often, student improvement is masked in a mathematical calculation (averaging) that makes reporting a student's current status next to impossible—past performances linger. We must consider that student achievement evidence from six months ago may not be reflective of where the student is today.

"It's February 17th. That means I'm doing a root canal. I always do root canals on February 17th!"

Education, like dentistry, is a people business. Dentists would never scope-and-sequence their patients' appointments. Dentists respond to the needs of their patients; we need to respond to the needs of our students. Some students master the content or skills long after the initial teaching date. We can no longer say to students that we've moved on. We must validate learning whenever it occurs, even if it is long after we taught it. Several strategies that allow us to do that are outlined in this book, but the first step is to be open—open to learning something new and finding a more effective way to fulfill our mission of helping every student maximize his or her potential. After all, a dentist would never tell a patient, "I'm sorry. I know you have a cavity, but we did fillings back in September. It's too late. We can't go back."

Being the Change

Being the change means taking a risk. While we can strategically plan what we do, the most important aspect of being the change is to take action. Some might argue in favour of exercising professional judgment, that we can't simply *try* every new idea without vetting it through our own personal experiences. Professional experience does matter in helping us sort out which practices are worth the effort and which we should ignore; however, when it comes to judging something to be a poor practice and lacking desire to change anything, the line can blur.

We spend too much time predicting how students are going to react to new practices or innovations without hearing from them. Sometimes these predictions are true, but other times they are simply an exercise in opting out because the person *doesn't want* to change anything. In subsequent chapters we discuss important changes we need to consider. The point here is to be open, to make professional judgments about what works, and to grow from the experience. "Try-learn-grow" is how we get better at anything we do, including teaching. Although the classroom is not necessarily an experimental lab, the best message we can send to our students is that we are still searching for the most effective and efficient ways to maximize their achievement and well-being.

Andrea DeVito is a middle school vice-principal who spent most of her career teaching high-school English. She recounts a time when she sought student feedback about her initial attempts using assessment for learning strategies in her English classes.

A few years ago I joined a group of teachers to collaborate on assessment *for* learning. We had all been working on changing our classroom assessment practices for awhile and felt that we had been doing a "pretty good" job of implementing several assessment *for* learning strategies. The question soon emerged: How do we know if what we are doing is working? As a group, we decided that we would do a survey with our students, giving them an opportunity to provide us with anonymous feedback (noting only student numbers), about how they were feeling about the learning environment in our classes.

The questions on the survey were designed as statements so that students had to rate their thoughts or feelings on a five-point scale, 1 being not very good and 5 being excellent. Statements ranged from "I feel valued as a student" to "I have multiple opportunities to self-assess" to "I receive frequent opportunities to improve my understanding." Each statement asked the students to give a rating for both how they felt in all of their classes, and then about how they felt about the class in which they were presented with the survey. The final question asked, "If you could be anywhere right at this moment, where would it be?" The intent of this question was to tease out insights into the student's interests, hobbies, favourite subjects, and so on.

Here's where it got personal. I handed out the surveys to all of my classes, but in my English 12 class I received the biggest "wake-up call." Once my Grade 12 students had completed the survey, they set to work on an in-class writing assignment. While they worked, I casually glanced through their responses, expecting to see that I was doing a fantastic job, and weren't these kids just so lucky to have such an open-minded, progressive teacher.

First—the responses were mixed—not a slew of "5s" by any means. But one of the surveys really stood out. Student #53049 had responded, under the "this class" column, with a litany of 1s. (That wasn't very good—I know, because I had to double-check.)

For the final question—If you could be anywhere right at this moment, where would it be?—the student's response was "Anywhere but in English class."

I scanned the class. Who is this student? This can't be right. Who of my lovely English 12 students could feel so negatively about this class, about my assessment and instructional practices, and about me? While I had my guesses, I couldn't be sure.

This, to me, necessitated the breaking of the anonymous code. I scanned the student numbers, and was shocked to find that it was "Kyle," a quiet, bright, A– student. I knew I needed to talk to Kyle privately about his responses on the survey.

Kyle and I had a chat. Turns out, his lowest grade was in English, and this grade was seriously compromising some of his scholarship opportunities. His frustration level in the course, and with his seeming inability to break 90 percent on a paper, was escalating at Mach speed. He wanted to improve his writing and was frustrated by the fact that my feedback to him was not providing him with the necessary guidance to do so.

We came to an agreement that he needed to revisit his essays, and that I needed to be more descriptive with my feedback so that he had a better understanding of what to do to improve.

After that day, my relationship with Kyle, and how Kyle felt about English class, improved tremendously. Most important, Kyle became a more confident, articulate writer, and he had the opportunity to break through his 90 percent.

Clearly, I needed a little self- and peer assessment as much as my students did.

Frustration can come in all shapes and sizes—and at all achievement levels. Andrea was not only open to receiving feedback from her students but willing to act upon that feedback to improve the classroom experience for every student, including Kyle. It is important to note that Andrea is an excellent teacher. She is a master of her curriculum, she develops exceptional relationships with her students, and she is a collaborative and supportive colleague. Her body of work throughout her career would have made it easy for her to pay little attention to what her students thought. However,

Andrea's willingness to be the change provided her with a crucial moment that forever solidified her commitment to implement effective assessment for learning strategies. While reflecting upon Andrea's story, we must all ask ourselves this question: *Is Andrea open to her students' feedback because she is an exceptional teacher, or is Andrea an exceptional teacher because she is open to receiving feedback from her students?*

Leaders don't wait for others to make the first move. Although many of the mission statements in schools mention something about developing *lifelong learners*, a few of the teachers in those schools have not learned much of anything new about their own profession since they were first hired. Yes, they've learned how to take attendance, print report cards, or fill out an office referral form, but they haven't learned anything new about the art of teaching.

Be the change strategically. Revamping your entire classroom practice all at once is not possible. As the saying goes, think big, but start small.

The question, then, is where to start.

Start with the greatest need. Examine the results of the students in your classroom to identify the greatest need. Note that once you have identified needs, resistance tends to be low since there is an identification that *something* must change, that there is a need for things to improve. Next, prioritize the needs. Once you have set priorities, you're ready to begin searching for the research-validated potential solutions to help meet your students' needs.

Being the change can be difficult, especially for teachers new to the profession or even new to a school. Change requires courage: the courage to be different in a profession that often thrives on uniformity. It requires the courage to stand out despite the staffroom politics and perceived hierarchy that can bring pressure, challenge, or even ridicule. When faced with a choice between protecting ourselves from ridicule or doing what's right for our students, we have to choose our students. The desire to help students is why we chose our profession. It's why we do what we do. Teaching is a way of life, a calling of higher purpose rather than simply a way to earn money to pay the bills. That calling compels us to do whatever it takes to help students achieve their best possible results. Parents entrust us with their children and expect us to educate them to the highest possible quality. Staying current is not a matter of choice, but a matter of professional responsibility.

Tips for Communicating with Parents

- Be up front with parents and students in communicating that you are a learner, too, and that if you learn about something that, you think, will create a more effective teaching and learning environment, then you will implement it, even in the middle of the year.

- Not every change you implement needs to be communicated in a formal manner. Through the various means of electronic communication, it is easier than ever to communicate with parents about what is happening in your class.

- If what you are changing is significant and represents a major shift in practice, then communicating in a more formal manner is a good idea. You might send a letter home or host a parent meeting.

- Whenever you change anything within your current practice, communicate with parents and students in a timely manner:
  - Explain *what* is changing so it's clear what will remain the same and what will be different.
  - Explain *why* something is changing—why will this change create a more effective learning environment?
  - Explain what will be different *after* the change. How will this change play out and what difference will students experience in the day-to-day classroom routines?
  - Explain how parents can provide support from home. Give parents a chance to be partners within the change process that you are bringing about.

Guiding Questions for Individuals or Learning Teams

1. Think of a time when you initiated a successful change (personally or professionally). What elements of that change made it successful?

2. Think of a time when you initiated a change (personally or professionally) that didn't last. What elements that could have made the change more successful were missing from the process?

3. Why do you think human beings "stoutly defend an established position despite overwhelming evidence against it"?

4. Based upon your experience, what are the key elements to successful, meaningful change within a classroom, school, or school district?

5. As you (individually, as a school, or as a district) embark on or continue your assessment and grading journey, what will you make sure is in place when moving ahead?

Suggested Readings for Further Study

While reading these resources will deepen your understanding of the change process, they will *not* help you to develop the personal courage necessary to "be the change."

- *Transforming Barriers to Assessment for Learning: Lessons Learned from Leaders* by Anne Davies, Sandra Herbst, and Beth Parrott Reynolds

- *Leading in a Culture of Change* by Michael Fullan

- *The Challenge of Change: Start School Improvement Now!* edited by Michael Fullan

- *Change Wars* edited by Andy Hargreaves and Michael Fullan

Chapter 2

Confidence Matters

Failure and success are not episodes, they are trajectories.

Rosabeth Moss Kanter

There is nothing more important to a student than confidence—
with it, students can learn anything; without it, they'll learn
nothing. While that statement may seem too definitive for some,
confidence is the key that unlocks the door to effort, persistence,
and learning for our students. If, as teachers, we do nothing more
than focus on building student confidence, we will create the kind
of learning environment that will allow our students to thrive.
Before we implement any of the strategies put forth in the rest of
this book, we need to create the conditions within our classrooms
that allow students to maximize their success.

Big Idea: Confidence as the Foundation of Success

Confidence is the sweet spot between arrogance and despair. Arrogance is the failure to see any weaknesses; despair is the failure to

acknowledge any strengths (Kanter, 2004). Arrogance will lead students to unfounded optimism, regardless of ability, effort, or even talent. With some students, it leads to a sense of entitlement where achievement and success are expected for all of the wrong reasons. Despair, on the other hand, leads students to feeling hopeless, as though all circumstances are plotting against them and there is no point in trying. When students reach this point, they are likely to disengage from the learning, and either emotionally or physically quit rather than put forth any effort. Either perspective is detrimental to student achievement.

When students are confident, they expect to succeed. This circumstance does not mean they will learn every lesson the first time it is taught; it does mean they believe they will learn the material being presented to them, even if it requires extra effort to do so. Confidence is the deciding factor on whether students learn. For decades, our collective belief was that the teacher decides when learning occurs. What we now know is that the students decide whether they are smart enough to learn and whether they have any hope for success if they try (Stiggins, 2004). If students believe that they *can* learn what is being taught and that success will be the eventual result of reasonable effort, then they will actively participate in the lesson. Without one or both of those beliefs, students are not ready to learn. As teachers, we decide the sequence of instruction, but the students control when learning occurs, and they base this decision on their own past record of success and failure. Confident students keep trying; the rest give up.

Reducing Anxiety

Unfortunately, anxiety has been the dominant emotion among a number of our students for decades. Some of that is typical in terms of human development; however, some of the anxiety students feel is avoidable. Rather than seeking to build confidence, we've inadvertently created learning environments and routines that raise anxiety and hamper students from performing at their best. While anxiety is a part of life and a normal emotion that most students learn to cope with, too much anxiety leads to poor performance and a loss of self-confidence.

A brief look at some issues associated with student anxiety makes it obvious that reducing anxiety is the first step to building student confidence. Elsie Chan (2001), an instructor teaching at the University of Victoria, identifies four problems associated with student anxiety:

1. Anxiety blocks normal thought processes. It interferes with memory, attention, and concentration which, in turn, leads to poor comprehension and poor results. With increased anxiety, students are at a disadvantage even before any instruction has occurred.

2. Anxiety encourages a passive approach to the material. Anxious students prefer to have the material fed to them as opposed to interacting with it. No risk is involved when students are told what to think, what to know, or what to consider important. Anxious students prefer to stay in their safe zone rather than stretch themselves as students.

3. Anxiety is associated with a general sense of incompetence. The passive approach is the result of a belief that a more active approach won't help. It is, in essence, a downward spiral. Passive students don't internalize the material, so they do poorly on assignments. Doing poorly reinforces the feeling of incompetence. It results in the students becoming even more passive when it comes to learning, which leads to even less internalization, which leads to more poor results. Eventually, such students give up.

4. Anxious students have little incentive to learn. Students are obligated to come to class because the course is required; however, anxious students are typically apathetic to the learning or produce the minimum to pass the course.

Knowing these ideas, how could we not focus on reducing anxiety? To be clear, teachers don't intend to raise student anxiety. On the contrary, most teachers strive to do the best they can for the students they teach. However, our traditional systems and structures, many of which will be addressed in later chapters, have set the conditions for stress, nervousness, and unreasonable pressure.

Our traditional practices can create an artificial competitiveness, for example, that works counter to student success. One such system is embedded within our practice of producing grades, and it reveals that we are still distracted from our true purpose.

Enabling Students to Focus on Learning

Confidence, not anxiety, is what students need. The belief that *I can learn* will provide students with the necessary strength in the face of some initial setbacks. Understanding that learning takes time and requires focused effort is critical to building confidence. While self-confidence is an internal emotion, emotions don't occur in a vacuum. Rather, emotions are often a response to the environment. Therefore, teachers play a vital role in setting up the conditions for success and allowing students to focus on learning rather than on managing their stress and using whatever means possible (dishonesty) to complete work and keep their grades afloat.

Each success a student has is evidence that success is possible. If you put together a few successes in a row, you have a winning streak. Kanter (2004) suggests that at the beginning of every winning streak, there is a leader who creates the foundation for confidence that permits unexpected people to achieve high levels of performance. We are the leaders in the classroom. We create the foundation for confidence that permits students to achieve at levels they never thought possible. That's our job as teachers: to build student confidence where the expectation of a positive result is the dominant emotion within each of our students.

Putting It into Practice

Teachers can make a positive difference to how their students face the future.

Teachers make a difference. Most individuals choose the teaching profession because they want to make a positive difference in the lives of the students they teach. A teacher's positive difference begins with reducing anxiety, building student confidence, and creating the conditions for success.

Unfortunately, the difference teachers make isn't always positive. If teachers have the ability to make the learning environment more supportive for students (which the vast majority do), then logic would suggest that they have an equal opportunity to make it worse. While making the learning environment worse is certainly not intentional, it can happen inadvertently through the decisions teachers make within their classrooms. Teachers can also lose sight of the reason they chose teaching as a profession.

We need only look at what happens to most students at the start of every school year to see how, without any purposeful effort, the conditions of success and failure replicate the previous year's results which, for some students, perpetuates the downward spiral.

The new school year usually brings new backpacks, binders, shoes, clothes, haircuts, friendships, and optimism—optimism that this is the year things will be different or better. Although they will never admit it, most students look forward to going back to school in the fall. The energy on the first day of school is unmistakable. There is usually a general sense of optimism, as the new school year provides students with the opportunity to start over.

While all of the newness is exciting, at the heart of the students' experience is what happens in the classroom and whether or not they can produce different or better results than the previous year. The peripheral newness and optimism is neutralized if a student's results are poor. Despite the new haircut, poor results will perpetuate the student's feeling that he or she is incompetent as a learner. This initial response can have a lasting effect throughout the year.

At some point, the losing streak has to be stopped. The optimum time for this is at the beginning of a school year or course. First impressions are lasting impressions; a student's first impression of how he or she will perform in a class, if negative, may not be reversible.

Over-preparing Students for Academic Victory

A way to control for this effect is to over-prepare students for their first evaluation. That is not to say we should make the assignment so easy that the students don't view it as real work. Rather, by waiting until we know students are ready to perform well, we can ensure a greater rate of success, validate the students' optimism, and set the conditions for academic winning streaks. If we simply forge ahead without being mindful of readiness, students who have a proven history of success will still succeed; however, students who lack that proven track record have a minimal chance of reversing their trajectory. For students, an academic victory early in the school year can set them up for a different trajectory.

What makes education so challenging is that our quest to find the most effective methods to teach never ends—the research never stops. This reality means that we must stay current and understand what society expects from its education system. The core mission of schools is evolving, and we need to stay aligned with this new purpose. Rick Stiggins (2004) suggests that our society has adopted a school mission that places educators clearly in the service of the success of *all* students. We now realize that if all schools sort students, then the bottom third of our student population will fail to develop essential reading, writing, and math proficiencies. While ranking and sorting of students may have once served a purpose, Stiggins suggests that this practice is no longer relevant.

Getting Beyond Complacency

With that new mission and the importance of each student completing high school with a minimal level of proficiency, it seems odd for us to predict that some students won't make it. While each school's history might show a number of students who did not finish high school, is it possible that this perspective allows us, at times, to become satisfied with a certain level of failure? Complacency is the first sign that we're not making a positive difference for all students. Teachers too often take credit for the successful students, but little responsibility for the failures. Early in my career, some students achieved high levels of success despite my limitations as a teacher. However, if we make a difference, then we need to make a difference to all.

In his book *Outliers*, Malcolm Gladwell (2008) suggests that success is far more than a product of ambition and intelligence. He recommends that we look *around* the successful people—that is, to the conditions under which they worked—to understand how success was achieved.

> Because we so profoundly personalize success, we miss opportunities to lift others onto the top rung. We make rules that frustrate achievement. We prematurely write off people as failures. We are too much in awe of those who succeed and far too dismissive of those who fail. And most of all, we become much too passive. We overlook just how large a role we all play—and by "we" I mean society—in determining who makes it and who doesn't. (pp. 32–33)

Have you ever prematurely written off a student as a failure? I'm embarrassed to admit that early on in my career, I did. To build confidence, we must first examine our structures, systems, policies, practices, routines, traditions, and habits. Success is not just about individual effort or talent—the conditions we set make more of a difference.

A teacher's job is to provide what Kanter (2004) refers to as the structure and the soul—the hard and the soft. We need to take responsibility for what she calls the big structures that serve as the cornerstones of confidence, and for the human touches that shape a positive emotional climate that inspires and motivates people—that's teaching. Our job is to structure our schools and classrooms with policies and processes that build confident learners and provide the necessary care and encouragement when that confidence waivers. With a positive emotional climate, students are capable of anything.

Taking a Leap of Faith

I wish I could point to a moment that began my assessment and grading journey, some magical moment where a professional epiphany was partnered with an instinctive drive toward what was right and just for all of my students. Unfortunately, I cannot. I look to a feeling of desperation as the pivotal moment in my career: a moment when my practices changed forever and my eyes were opened to what's really important when making a difference for all students.

In 2004, as vice-principal of McNicoll Park Middle School in Penticton, British Columbia, I had a part-time teaching assignment. Headed into my fourteenth year in education, I had experience teaching every grade level from 6 to 12 in various subjects, including English, language arts, physical education, social studies, and math. In 2004, my teaching assignment was exclusively Grade 8 math. In our timetable, math occurred every day, all year, for 48 minutes.

I knew I was a good teacher—not to say I was the best, most dynamic, or most inspiring. While balancing administrative duties with classroom responsibilities, I felt my commitment to my teaching was as strong as ever. I knew what good teaching looked like. At least that's what I thought, until I met "Chris."

Chris was a student in one of my math classes that year. During September, which for math is typically more review than new, Chris was doing okay. By his standards, he had done relatively well in Grade 7, so Chris was fairly comfortable. While he wasn't a frequent flyer to the office, he was far from a model student. His behaviours were challenging both in and out of the classroom, and he was often off-task or not paying attention at all. He was a nice boy—we got along quite well—but like most 14-year-old boys, he was distracted and prepared to put in only the minimal effort necessary to get by. With all of that, Chris managed to make it through September in decent shape. By the middle of October, however, it became obvious that Chris was losing interest in math and was beginning to disengage from school. Once we ventured into the new curriculum, Chris was lost, and I was losing faith in my ability as a teacher.

Chris sat at the front of the room. I wanted him close to me both to benefit his learning and to keep him on task. For most students, the fact I was vice-principal carried enough weight that they were compliant, attentive, and focused while in my class. For most students, that is, except Chris. As we moved through October, Chris's body language and sporadic attendance made it clear that he had no interest in math. If there was a way to get out of doing the work, he would find it, use it, and store it in the toolbox. He rarely paid attention to the lesson and never completed any practice work in class or any homework. For the first time in my career, I didn't have an answer, and I was desperate to find it.

In my search, I began to explore *new* ideas of assessment for learning. After reading numerous articles, attending a few conferences, and reading several books, I decided to try something: a more detailed unit plan that identified specific learning targets, as well as their underpinnings, in student-friendly language. I detail the specifics of this in Chapter 3, but for the purposes of building student confidence, what I experienced with Chris was remarkable. Although I don't believe we are one tool away from a miracle, what happened to Chris was close. The use of student-friendly language helped Chris to understand the overarching concepts he was to learn and the underpinnings that would lead him to that mastery. By becoming aware of the underpinnings of the learning targets (e.g., knowing the definitions of squares and square roots *before* using the Pythagorean formula to calculate the third side of a right triangle), Chris recognized that there were some concepts in math he knew, after all.

As we began to use that list as a sort of checklist for students to track their learning, Chris's confidence began to grow, and so did mine. The issue wasn't that Chris knew nothing about math; it was that I hadn't made math accessible to him. Chris had no way of knowing what he already knew since he didn't really understand what we were learning. Let me be clear: I am not suggesting that one tool will reverse a trajectory of losing, but we are all definitely one new practice away from beginning to shift the tone within our classes from anxiety to confidence.

■ ■ ■

Chris's reversal took a major leap of faith on both our parts. I had to trust the research and believe that what it said was effective would work. Chris had to trust that this new way of working within my class was worth a fresh start. While I found implementing all of the "stuff"—the new practices of assessment, instruction, and grading—professionally rewarding, it was Chris's personal changes in motivation and confidence that inspired me the most.

Many of the things that *matter* within this book are the things I began to infuse into my classroom practice. Now, more than seven years later, I have a greater depth of knowledge and appreciation for the way in which these *things* can change the learning environment within the classroom. As I started to use more frequent formative assessment to understand where my students were, I could identify (with Chris) what he understood and where he needed more support. I began to use descriptive feedback to set out what he understood, where he needed extra support, and what his next steps should be. While I certainly had limited experience with differentiated instruction, I now realize that I was attending to Chris's specific learning needs by adapting and adjusting lessons to bring him through the lessons.

Building Relationships

Later that year, I began to think about how I graded, why students needed practice, and how improvement could play a role in accurately reflecting where Chris was within his own learning continuum. All the while, I was trying to lead Chris to a point where *he* took some ownership over his learning. My experience in these areas was extremely limited and the implementation of these ideas was neither simultaneous nor flawless. For the most part, I was *thinking* about all of these things and trying to make sense of how they could transform my classroom. My journey was in its infancy, but I was willing to take my first step. My efforts, however flawed they might have been, paid immediate dividends when it came to Chris's disposition and confidence around math.

"Jennifer," a friend of Chris's, saw first-hand the changes. She was an excellent student who took school seriously. She was as deeply rooted with the cool kids as Chris was, but for Jennifer, doing well in school was also socially acceptable. On more than one occasion, Jennifer told me how discouraged and frustrated Chris was with math. However, when I began changing everything about how I taught, Jennifer began to see a change in Chris. One day after class, she went out of her way to tell me that Chris tried *really hard* on his homework the previous night and that he had called her for help on a few algebra questions. Jennifer added that Chris had *never* done homework before and had certainly never asked someone else for help.

At that moment I realized I had stumbled on to something. Not an expert, I thought only that I had finally caught a break. I couldn't see seven years ahead and know that I would be writing about my experience with Chris. I remember feeling so relieved that I might have a chance to salvage Chris's year. The cumulative impact of everything I tried to do enabled Chris to reconnect to school and renew his motivation in a way I could not have expected. What I implemented in my first year benefited many more students than just Chris, but typical of most teachers, I was focused on finding a way to bring my lowest achiever back to a world of hope and possibility.

Assessment for learning and sound grading practices are really about relationships. Whether you are in the early stages of trying something new or are solidifying your commitment to your new practices, the unexpected results are the changed relationships you'll develop with your students. Education is a human business, and with that comes a responsibility to nurture the relationships we have with our students. My relationship with Chris improved beyond expectations. He was on time and attentive, which allowed me to let down my guard and focus on instruction rather than management. Chris and I reconnected as people. We could talk about things *other* than math. Through the various strategies I implemented that year, Chris and I worked together to ensure his success.

Providing Opportunities for Success

The relationship that developed between me and Chris paid dividends. At the start of Chris's Grade 8 year, I had thought that Chris was the epitome of a student headed for drop out. In September 2008, as fate would have it, I was assigned to be vice-principal at Penticton Secondary School, the school that students from McNicoll Park Middle School transitioned to. Chris was entering Grade 12 and was on track to graduate. I don't take credit for that—Chris deserves the credit—and many teachers and a long-term collective effort were required to get him there. However, I would argue that if the 2004–05 school year had played out differently, his other teachers may never have had the chance. If I had carried on the way I started, I doubt Chris would have completed Grade 8 and made it through high school. He had other teachers in Grade 8, but I found out later that math was the subject that gave him the most difficulty and was most often the reason he chose not to attend school.

During his Grade 12 year, Chris showed unmistakable maturity and confidence. Our relationship was revived and, while we never spoke about Grade 8 math (much to his delight, I'm sure), I was grateful to see who he had become. At one point, the wheelchair of one of our students broke. Our shop teacher suggested that Chris fix it. After a few simple instructions from his teacher, Chris took the wheelchair into the adjacent shop and repaired it with ease, something I never imagined would have been possible when he was in my Grade 8 class.

We shouldn't predict where students will end up, especially students who struggle in school. One perspective suggests that students struggle because they lack the ability or are not putting forth enough effort. Another perspective, however, suggests that students struggle because they have not been given the opportunity to excel. While students with learning disabilities or intellectual limitations struggle because it is not possible for them to reach the expected level of performance, so many other students struggle because they need the opportunity to succeed in an environment that creates the optimum conditions for success.

Cindy Russill is a special education and learning assistance teacher who has worked at every level K–12. Cindy has seen first-hand the impact that many of these new practices have had on her students. As she often points out, she sees the students *after* they have left their classes and are faced with the numerous and diverse assignments, projects, and learning activities that teachers have assigned. She witnesses, first-hand, anxiety, frustration, and hopelessness as her students grapple with why they don't "get it." In recent years, however, Cindy has also witnessed a sense of optimism and hope from some of the students: those whose teachers have created the conditions for success by implementing some of the strategies and practices discussed in this book. Most interesting is that the same student might feel confident about one class and pessimistic about another. This difference in confidence is the result of different practices and routines being employed by different teachers.

Cindy's students confide in her, admitting that there are only certain classes for which they are willing to take academic risks. These *certain classes* are the ones in which her students feel that success, even partial success, is possible, and that if it isn't, there is a support plan in place. One student told Cindy that her social studies class was the only class she studied for because it was the only class for which she knew *how* to study. Another student admitted to Cindy that he hadn't studied for an upcoming test. When asked why, the student said the teacher hadn't told the class what was going to be on the test. Cindy knew that was not true and that the teacher had provided an outline for what was to be on the test. When confronted with this fact, the student responded by telling Cindy that the teacher didn't do it in a way that made sense or that he could understand—even our best intentions can fall flat with some of our students.

How Confidence Relates to Academic Effort

For Cindy's students, the issue of confidence is paramount. In her words, "students are more willing to take risks in different subjects based on how confident they are in achieving success." The obvious connection for her was that the classrooms where the conditions changed to reflect the current research on assessment, instruction, and grading were the classes in which her students *tried harder* and *persisted longer* when facing academic obstacles. No one epitomized this more than a student named Cody, with whom Cindy had worked through four years of high school.

Cody, a student diagnosed with a learning disability, struggled in school from an early age. Throughout elementary and middle school, Cody's academic struggles worsened. Both he and his mother reached a point toward the end of middle school where Cody refused to do any work. His mother described the nightly homework routine as unbearable. The tension and anxiety mounted as Cody would sit at the table with his eyes closed, refusing to do anything. Punishments and consequences made no difference; Cody was not going to complete his assignments. As he moved through middle school, his mother was less able to assist him, especially with math.

As Cody entered Grade 9, his mother expected that things would be virtually the same, only "bigger and worse." She felt his chances of making it through high school were "slim to none." As the pressure mounted in Grade 9, Cody's negative behaviours began to emerge. He just didn't care. His apathy toward school was now paired with an aggressive disposition that led to fights with other students, something that at a younger age would have been seen as out of character. Cody's relationship with his mother deteriorated, and they were both frustrated by his experiences at school. He wanted a bare minimum to pass. If he didn't think he could pass, then he didn't try at all. From Cody's perspective, it was better to save face than look stupid.

At the time Cody entered Grade 10, many of his teachers were beginning to shift their thinking around assessment, instruction, and grading. Some were allowing students to rewrite tests and assignments, some were breaking down the learning outcomes into student-friendly language, and some were exploring how to incorporate practice and improvement into their grading. All of this led to a mind shift in Cody, which helped him realize that a poor performance on any task was no longer final—there were opportunities to relearn and redo. It is interesting to note that Cody's mind shift began as he realized he was being held accountable for the expected learning in his classes. Many of his teachers no longer accepted that some of the work wouldn't be done; it was not okay to omit portions of the learning and receive a zero. While Cody initially resisted the shift, eventually he realized that it was going to take more effort to avoid the work.

Another unexpected outcome of the changes was how Cody's relationships with his teachers were transformed. As was addressed earlier in this chapter, the new practices and routines fostered a new kind of relationship between Cody and his teachers, a relationship that clearly put Cody's success as the priority. In the past, Cody would make it difficult for any of his teachers to develop a positive relationship. All of that changed as Cody began to see his teachers not as enemies, but as people who truly cared about his success. This shift in his relationships with his teachers was, according to Cindy, the glue that held the transformation together. As a result, Cody's anxiety over school was replaced by a growing confidence that success might be possible. The conditions in the classrooms were creating a new outlook on learning for Cody—an outlook that motivated him beyond *just passing* to achieving the highest possible grade.

The Power of Confidence

By Grade 11, Cody took courses that, he admits, pushed him beyond what he thought he was capable of, chemistry, physics, and history among them. However, he had a greater sense of confidence and possibilities; he didn't just want to pass—he was now pushing himself to excel. Not only did his achievement improve to an Honour Roll level, but he was doing it while enrolled in courses that seemed unlikely just two years earlier. As his achievement improved, his negative behaviours subsided, and he became a positive member of the school community again.

While not every student will accomplish as rapid a turnaround as Cody, we can never underestimate the power that confidence has over our students. More than anything, students want to know we care. We reveal our priorities not by what we say, but by what we do. If we focus on promoting confidence and a positive emotional climate, and on developing healthy relationships, our students will have the desire to achieve things they have not yet experienced.

Later chapters will outline effective classroom practices; however, never lose sight of the changed emotional response students have to those practices. Early in my career I did the opposite of almost everything set forth in this book. I know the practices outlined in this book work both because I've experienced them for myself and because I saw how the opposite practices failed to support the achievement of all my students. Even so, it is important to remember that the tools and practices are just the *stuff*—the students are why we do it!

Confidence is about the big picture—it's about developing a lifelong mindset that will carry students throughout their academic careers. Confidence is the ultimate gift we can give a student. Rather than simply having my students learn a subject, I want to build their confidence so that they always expect success and their ability to cope with challenges comes from an optimism embedded within their habitual ways of thinking.

Tips for Communicating with Parents

- Clearly communicate with parents that you are focusing on building student confidence.

- Communicate frequently to build the parents' confidence in you as a teacher.

- Make sure parents know *why* changes are being made. If the *why* is presented in a way that is logical, fair, and reasonable, and that seeks to reduce anxiety, parents will develop confidence in you and feel that you truly have the best interest of their children in mind.

Guiding Questions for Individuals or Learning Teams

1. Reflect on your current practices and routines. Which ones raise student confidence to a level where success is expected?

2. Which of your current practices and routines do you think has the greatest potential to disproportionately raise student anxiety to the point where success is compromised?

3. Have you ever been on a personal losing streak? What helped you turn it around?

4. Have you ever had a student similar to Chris? What was the most effective thing you did in developing that student into a confident learner?

5. What is self-confidence and how would you recognize it in your students? What would you see your students doing? What would you hear your students saying?

Suggested Readings for Further Study

- *The 7 Habits of Highly Successful People* by Stephen R. Covey
- *Outliers: The Story of Success* by Malcolm Gladwell
- *Confidence: How Winning Streaks and Losing Streaks Begin and End* by Rosabeth Moss Kanter
- *Activating the Desire to Learn* by Bob Sullo

Chapter 3

Assessment Accuracy Matters

> *The time has come to take advantage of this new understanding of the potential of assessment and to fundamentally rethink the relationship between assessment practices and effective schools.*
>
> **Rick Stiggins**

Assessment *accuracy* comes when we are clear about the purpose for the assessment, the specific learning that is being assessed, and the method with which we intend to assess the learning. At its core, assessment for learning is a process, not necessarily an event or tool, whereby students and teachers can fully identify where individual students are along the learning continuum. As a result, students are clearer on their individual strengths and challenges, and teachers have more reliable information with which to make decisions about the next steps in instruction. Without this information, students are left out of the instructional decision-making process, only able to guess why lessons are relevant, and teachers risk making misguided decisions that produce inefficient and ineffective instructional design.

Accuracy matters because time is limited. We always run out of time before we run out of textbook, so decisions and choices about the next steps in instruction are already being made in classrooms across North America. With assessment accuracy, these decisions are more informed and serve the students' learning needs in a more meaningful way.

Whether an assessment is summative or formative, accuracy matters. Regardless of purpose, assessments must produce accurate information to clearly inform teachers and students about the next steps to improvement, or others outside the classroom about the kind of progress a student is making. We need to know what to do next or be able to accurately reflect the progress achieved so far. While I will emphasize accuracy from a *formative* perspective, accuracy overall is critical to achieving a balanced assessment system. Although I have learned about *assessment accuracy* from a variety of sources, I must acknowledge, up front, that my primary source of knowledge and understanding is the leadership and work of the Assessment Training Institute in Portland, Oregon.

Big Idea: Accurate Assessment for Student Success

While the distinction between summative and formative assessment is not new, our collective renewed interest in formative assessment can be traced back to Paul Black and Dylan Wiliam's 1998 article, "Inside the Black Box: Raising Standards Through Classroom Assessment." As part of the Assessment Reform Group in the United Kingdom, Black and Wiliam conducted a meta-analysis of over a decade's worth of previous research on the use of formative assessment. In the article, Black and Wiliam provide a synthesis of how the use of formative assessment practices (assessment for learning) can raise standards, improve student morale, and, most important, produce achievement gains unmatched by any other practice. While not proclaiming it a *magic bullet* for education, Black and Wiliam put forth a compelling argument as to why formative assessment is an essential component to maximizing student success.

Almost simultaneously, Rick Stiggins and the Assessment Training Institute (Portland, Oregon) brought forth the idea of a *new mission* for schools. That new mission's focus is on creating a balanced assessment system within our schools: one that strikes a balance between tests *of* learning and classroom assessment *for* learning (Stiggins, 2004). In addition, the new mission focuses on students developing minimal competencies in all of their essential learning, but primarily in their core subjects.

The Focusing Role of Assessment for Learning

This second piece was in response to the increase in accountability through standardized testing throughout the United States.
By using assessment *for* learning on a day-to-day basis in the classroom, teachers would better prepare students to meet the standards on most year-end, standardized tests; they would be breaking down the essential learning within each subject and scaffolding their instruction to meet the students' needs. Stiggins and others realized that standardized tests are not likely to go away anytime soon, so the question was how best to prepare students for those tests. Students would be better prepared, Stiggins suggested, if they understood clearly the learning outcomes or intentions and their progress in relation to those learning intentions, and were guided through specific activities to help close that gap. A teacher's lessons would become more purposeful, focused, and specific to individual student needs.

Both the Assessment Reform Group (United Kingdom) and the Assessment Training Institute (Oregon) reintroduced educators to the ideas of assessment for learning and the potential power it has when used appropriately in a classroom on a day-to-day basis.

What followed was a renewed interest in formative assessment that produced compelling research and powerful processes from the likes of Ken O'Connor, Anne Davies, Thomas Guskey, Ruth Sutton, Jay McTighe, Michael Scriven, Lorna Earl, Damien Cooper, Grant Wiggins, and Rob Marzano.

The research was clear, the results were compelling, and the action was simple—simple in the sense that it was obvious what would improve student achievement. The complexity, as discussed in Chapter 1, pertained to the unwillingness of some individual educators to change their current practices to what was validated by research. In other cases, what appeared to be unwillingness was really an issue of not clearly understanding what assessment for learning looks like in the classroom. It isn't so much an understanding of *what* to do; it is more an issue of *how* to do it. By knowing the assessment purpose, outcomes, and methods, however, teachers will have an improved sense of how to begin.

Knowing the Purpose of Assessment

The purpose of summative assessment is to inform others, primarily parents, about the learning progress their children have made. This verification occurs at the end of a predetermined learning cycle—a unit, a term, a year—and is designed to produce the grade that students have earned on an assignment, exam, or report card. These assessments of learning are necessary moments throughout the school year where the primary goal is to check student status against the learning outcomes established by the prescribed curriculum. Often, the cumulative effect of the assessments *of* learning is to substantiate the learning by students and to validate the collective progress made by individual schools or school districts. Summative assessments occur after learning has taken place; formative assessments, before.

The fundamental difference between assessments *of* and *for* learning is what will happen with the results. If the intent of the assessment is to report to others, then, as previous outlined, the assessment is primarily summative—a learning verification tool. If, however, the purpose of the assessment is to report internally, that is, to inform students and teachers internally about student progress and preparation, then the assessment is formative. While almost any assessment instrument can be used for summative or formative purposes, some, by design, are better suited to summative use and others to formative use (Chappuis & Chappuis, 2007–2008). How the assessment results are used determines whether an assessment is summative or formative.

Assessment *for* learning occurs when there is still time for students to make improvements before the summative event. The feedback that students receive allows them, along with the teacher, to take action before verification of learning is necessary.

> Assessments for learning happen while learning is still underway. These are assessments that we conduct throughout teaching and learning to diagnose student needs, plan our next steps in instruction, provide students with feedback they can use to improve the quality of their work, and help students feel in control of their journey to success. Each one reveals to students increments of achievement and how to do better the next time. On these occasions, the grading function is laid aside. This is not about accountability—those are assessments of learning. This is about getting better. (Stiggins, Arter, Chappuis, & Chappuis, 2009, p. 31)

Knowing the purpose sets the instructional paradigm from which all future instructional decisions will be made. In subsequent chapters, we will discuss the importance of descriptive feedback, student involvement, practice, and improvement, none of which would factor into instruction without knowing why we need to gather information about student success while they are still learning. Knowing the purpose clarifies the decisions, strategies, processes, and instruction necessary to maximize student success. Our purpose ultimately comes from knowing *why* we need assessment information and *who* is going to use it.

Knowing What We're Looking For

Once we know *why* we are assessing, the focus then shifts to *what* we and our students are looking for. Identifying clear learning targets for each curricular outcome simplifies our ability to pinpoint what we are looking for. Students also benefit, as they will now understand what it is they are supposed to learn. They gain a clear picture of both the bigger learning goals and the underpinnings that make comprehension more likely. Every curriculum guide identifies the key learning outcomes for a subject. Some of the outcomes represent basic knowledge, while others represent a higher level of thinking or problem solving. Once the level of thinking can be determined, we can then identify the underpinnings necessary for students to achieve the larger learning goal (a point that will be further emphasized later in the chapter). By grouping the learning targets by type—knowledge, reasoning, skill, as well as products and disposition (Stiggins, Arter, Chappuis, & Chappuis, 2009)—students more clearly understand the sequence of learning. The following table identifies and explains key learning targets:

1. **Knowledge Targets:** Represent the basic knowledge facts that need to be learned or memorized. In some cases, students will be allowed to retrieve this information using reference material.

   Examples: vocabulary lists, multiplication facts, identification of types of triangles, recalling of procedural steps

2. **Reasoning Targets:** Identify what students are *to do* with the knowledge they have gained. These targets represent their *thinking* proficiencies.

   Examples: comparing and contrasting two characters, evaluating an opinion, interpreting data sets

3. **Performance Targets:** Identify what needs to be *seen* or *heard*. These are demonstration targets where *doing* is more important than just *knowing*.

   Examples: reading fluently, shooting a basketball, playing the trumpet, conducting a science experiment

4. **Product Targets:** Represent a final product that is produced from the student's ability to *know*, *think*, and *do*.

   Examples: writing, drawing, mapping, reporting, creating a personal plan or a fitness plan

5. **Disposition Targets:** Identify important *affective* goals that are by-products of the students' learning experience.

   Examples: reading for pleasure, increasing appreciation for classical music, enjoying volleyball playing

Source: Adapted from *Classroom Assessment for Student Learning: Doing It Right—Using It Well* by Rick Stiggins, Judith Arter, Jan Chappuis, and Stephen Chappuis (New York, NY: Allyn & Bacon, 2009).

By making the targets clear for students, we

- give meaning and relevance to the bigger standards or learning outcomes in our curriculum guides

- identify the steps in learning necessary to reach those larger goals

- identify for parents what their children will be learning

Knowing How to Find What We're Looking For

Once we know why and what we are assessing, the final piece to accuracy is identifying *how* to assess the targets in the most efficient and effective way. Efficiency and effectiveness are important because we need to collect enough evidence to verify that learning is progressing without wasting valuable instructional minutes by *over*-assessing or teaching targets and lessons the students may have already mastered.

The first challenge is to avoid favouring one method of assessment. While balancing formative and summative assessments is important, using a variety of methods to assess student progress is also important. Certain targets lend themselves to certain methods of assessment; however, there are times when teachers over-rely on one particular method (e.g., multiple choice), which leads to a limited view of student progress or success. Using assessment methods that match the learning targets being assessed provides clear information about the progress students are making.

All along, whether from researchers or implementers, the message has been *balance*—establish a balanced assessment process or system.

Educators, however, tend to swing the assessment pendulum from one extreme to the other, especially early on in their assessment journey. When initially introduced to the ideas of authentic and accurate formative assessments, educators often discontinue the use of "traditional" assessment methods, such as multiple choice or short answer; instead, they try to use a performance scale or criterion-based rubric to assess everything.

The reality is that all assessment methods have their place in a balanced assessment process, but the learning target needs to be matched with the assessment method that will most accurately allow the students to show what they know. In his *Assessment Manifesto*, Stiggins (2008) calls for the development of productive assessment systems that serve the needs of a wide variety of assessment users.

> …such systems acknowledge that a wide variety of decision makers need access to different kinds of information in different forms at different times to help students learn. If any of these users' needs are ignored, or they are provided misinformation due to inept assessments, ineffective decisions will result that will harm student confidence, motivation, and learning, as well as student and teacher efficacy. (p. 4)

Once the learning targets are identified, the key is to match them to assessment methods. Most assessment methods are relatively effective with most learning targets; however, there are a few mismatches. Below are three common mismatches related to learning targets and assessment methods.

1. **Assessing knowledge targets using performance assessments.** Using performance assessment for knowledge-level targets is inefficient, given other methods that are available. For example, if students are expected to know the meaning of 25 key vocabulary terms for their science unit on photosynthesis, the most efficient assessment method is either short answer or written responses. To use a performance method is too time consuming. Knowledge level targets often represent the building block from which performance skills are demonstrated later on in the learning. To ensure that the prerequisite knowledge has been acquired, we must use more effective methods. In short, a teacher is not going to ask students to perform the science vocabulary words.

2. **Assessing reasoning targets using multiple-choice questions.** Reasoning targets take students beyond simple knowledge to a place of explanation. When asked to reason, students are often expected to analyze, compare, contrast, classify, or summarize. While this list isn't exhaustive, it reveals the fundamental idea that using multiple-choice questions to assess a student's ability to summarize is, at best, limited and, at worst, ineffective. While short answer questions could be used to assess simple patterns of reasoning, using short answer to assess a student's ability to reason is definitely not a good match.

3. **Assessing skills using short answer or written responses.** Performance skills need to be seen or heard in order to be accurately assessed. Using short answer questions to know whether a student can speak fluently in French or serve a volleyball would not provide any accuracy. While the knowledge of French vocabulary or the specific techniques to serve a volleyball could be assessed using short answer, the demonstration of skill cannot be.

By knowing why, what, and how students will be assessed, we can more accurately identify where each student is along his or her own learning continuum. In other words, we need to do the following:

- Determine whether we are reporting out or reporting in (why).

- Identify the learning targets, and their underpinnings, in a student-friendly format so students have a clear picture of what the intended learning is (what).

- Choose methods to assess those targets and underpinnings that most efficiently and effectively identify whether the students have achieved what they were supposed to have achieved (how).

With assessment accuracy, we get not only a clear picture of what has been achieved, but a blueprint for what future instruction is required to close any gaps between the desired learning and the learning revealed by the assessments; students gain the same insight about themselves. Making instructional decisions with our formative assessment results is the fundamental purpose behind using assessment for learning strategies. (Instructional decisions are discussed in Chapter 5.) Formative assessments lead to more informed instruction, which, in turn, leads to greater achievement by students. Choosing our methods strategically brings a balanced, accurate assessment process that maximizes our instructional minutes and increases students' ability to succeed.

Putting It into Practice

Checking to see whether students know the underpinnings of learning outcomes benefits both teachers and students.

Figure 3.1 (see next page) represents where I started. In fact, it represents the first thing I ever developed once I had learned about the power of assessment for learning and how it could transform my classroom. After my first assessment *for* learning experience at the Assessment Training Institute in Portland, Oregon, I immediately went to work developing and implementing the new ideas I had come home with. Chris, a student I referred to in Chapter 2, was a member of the class in which this tool was first introduced. It was fundamental to changing Chris's paradigm around his own abilities as a student.

This Measurement Unit Plan identifies two main learning outcomes. These targets, or outcomes, were taken from the British Columbia Integrated Learning Resource for Grade 8 math. These learning outcomes, as with most curriculum guides, were written by math teachers for math teachers. Put any curriculum guide in front of students, however, and they likely won't understand the phrasing or how to demonstrate the intended learning. Clear learning outcomes, or targets, means breaking down the intended learning into student-friendly language. While this document is primarily a preview of the unit of study, it evolved into a checklist for students to verify their own learning through the use of *I can* statements.

Adopting Student-Friendly Language

While demonstrating the application of the Pythagorean theorem, perimeter, area, and circumference are the primary outcomes of this measurement unit, there are underpinnings of those skills that students need to know before success in the calculations is possible. For example, students can't use the Pythagorean relationship unless they know what squares and square roots are, what a right triangle is, and how to identify the hypotenuse. While these underpinnings might seem too simple for some, teachers begin to lose students early in the learning process when they assume that students already know these essential elements. Many of the underpinnings are simple and easy to assess, but they must be assessed to maximize the effectiveness of the forthcoming lessons. By making the targets clear for students, we give meaning and relevance to the bigger standards or learning outcomes in our curriculum guides, we identify the steps in learning, and we identify for parents what their children are going to learn.

Figure 3.1: Measurement Unit Plan for Grade 8 Math

Learning Target #1

Use the Pythagorean relationship to calculate the measure of the third side of a triangle, given the other two sides in a two-dimensional application.

Student Friendly Learning Target Statements

Knowledge Targets *"What I need to know!"*	❏ I can explain the definition of squares and square roots. ❏ I can identify the hypotenuse on a right triangle. ❏ I can explain the Pythagorean theorem.
Reasoning Targets *"What I can do with what I know"*	❏ I can identify a right triangle. ❏ I can predict the approximate value of imperfect squares and square roots. ❏ I can summarize when and how the Pythagorean theorem could be applied in "real-life" situations.
Skill Targets *"What I can demonstrate"*	❏ I can calculate squares and square roots. ❏ I can use the Pythagorean theorem to calculate the length of the hypotenuse of a right triangle when given the lengths of the other two sides. ❏ I can use the Pythagorean theorem to calculate the length of an unknown side of a right triangle when given the lengths of the hypotenuse and another side.

■ ■ ■

Figure 3.1 (continued)

Product Targets *"What I can make to show my learning"*	❏ I can construct a three-dimensional model that both proves the Pythagorean theorem and demonstrates its "real-life" application.

Learning Target #2

Describe the patterns and generalize the relationships by determining the areas and perimeters of quadrilaterals and the areas and circumferences of circles.

Estimate and calculate the area of composite figures.

Student Friendly Learning Target Statements

Knowledge Targets *"What I need to know!"*	❏ I can explain what a quadrilateral is. ❏ I can explain perimeter, area, and circumference. ❏ I can identify the different formulas used to calculate perimeter, area, and circumference. ❏ I can explain what a polygon is.
Reasoning Targets *"What I can do with what I know"*	❏ I can classify polygons based upon the number of sides. ❏ I can compare and contrast quadrilaterals, squares, and rectangles, and parallelograms. ❏ I can translate word problems into a mathematical formula to calculate the correct answer.
Skill Targets *"What I can demonstrate"*	❏ I can calculate the perimeter of any object, given the lengths of each side of the figure. ❏ I can find the length of an unknown side of a figure when given the perimeter and the lengths of the remaining sides. ❏ I can calculate the area of a rectangle and of a square. ❏ I can calculate the area of a parallelogram. ❏ I can calculate the area of a triangle.

■ ■ ■

Figure 3.1 (continued)

Skill Targets *"What I can demonstrate"*	❑ I can calculate the area of a circle. ❑ I can calculate the area of composite figures.

Product Targets *"What I can make to show my learning"*	❑ I can design and draw a floor plan for a small vacation home and do the following:
	  – Determine the type of flooring you can afford given the size of the main floor
	  – Determine the amount of fencing you need in order to enclose your yard
	  – Draw a diagram of the front of your house and determine the total amount of siding needed to cover it

While *disposition targets* are not listed in the Measurement Unit Plan (Figure 3.1), it is important to identify them or at least have them permeate everything surrounding your instruction. They might be relevant to the unit of study. A disposition for all of my lessons, no matter what I was teaching, was for students to gain a greater appreciation for the subject, topic, or process of the day. We don't just want to teach students how to read; we want them to learn to love reading and sometimes choose it as a leisure activity. I didn't just want my students to understand the math they were learning—I wanted them to learn to *like* math just a bit more. I was realistic in knowing that not every student in my class would *love* math, but I was hopeful that I could move them along the continuum.

The Underpinnings of Confidence

What I did not anticipate was how favourably students, especially Chris, would react to this one tool. As we proceeded through the unit of study, the growth in the students' confidence to *do* math was astonishing. As teachers, we understand that the underpinnings of the larger learning outcomes are quite simple and don't usually spend much time assessing them. For students, however, the student-friendly learning targets and their underpinnings produce a very different reaction.

At the beginning of the unit, I had the students *self-assess* their background knowledge in the areas of study. Though not realizing it at the time, I was informally assessing where students were and how I might fill in the gaps before any new learning began. What was great to see was that every student could check off at least one or two things on the list. We know that not all underpinnings are created equal. As teachers, we know that *performing* the calculations of Pythagoras will play a much larger role in the final analysis than being able to identify a hypotenuse. The students, however, do not realize that. They later come to recognize it on the unit test and other summative assessments, but in the initial stages of the unit, that does not matter. What matters the most is that every student can check off *something*.

Almost immediately, as Chris checked off a few of the boxes, I could hear him say to Jennifer, "Hey, I do know some stuff. Maybe I don't suck at Math." Identifying the targets is as much about student psychology as it is about learning. Chris realized, through this example, that he did have some math knowledge. My job was to let him know that whatever was missing was my responsibility to help correct. Chris's job was to remain focused on improvement and, together, we would ensure his continued improvement. Throughout the unit, I had the students take out that unit plan and self-assess their level of mastery on each of the topics. As students checked each of the boxes beside the targets, I began to hear several atypical conversations throughout my classroom: students talked about how much they knew, what they had improved on, and what they needed to do next to reach a higher level. Figure 3.1 does not represent a confidence builder in and of itself. However, the tool (and the routines that surround it) set the conditions to shift the learning paradigm and develop confidence in students who were otherwise intimidated by math.

Assessing Student Readiness

Lisa West, a math teacher at Penticton Secondary School, developed a simple, yet effective, method of pre-assessment that accurately identifies student readiness in Trigonometry.

At the beginning of her unit, Lisa projects an image of a right triangle on the screen (see Figure 3.2); she then asks the class a series of questions about this triangle.

Each student is given three cards, one with *A*, one with *B*, and one with *C*. Lisa asks a question and prompts the students to hold up the card that they feel is the correct answer. Below are examples of the questions she asks:

1. Which side is the opposite of angle β?

2. Which side is adjacent to angle θ?

3. SIN β is (a) A over B, (b) A over C, or (c) B over C?

As students raise their cards, Lisa sees within an instant where the collective knowledge is and what needs correcting. After each answer, she asks a student who chose the correct answer to justify his or her answer. More often than not, the students who are incorrect are reminded of their error and don't make the same mistake again. Furthermore, Lisa can identify which students are consistently getting the answer incorrect. By spending extra time with those students, she corrects their mistakes, helps reinforce a little more knowledge, and brings them up to speed and ready for new instruction.

Figure 3.2

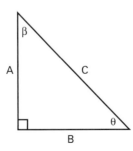

When you examine Lisa's routine, you realize that she knew her purpose (formative), which targets she was assessing (revealed through her questions), and which method (three cards) would be the most efficient in gathering this information. This whole exercise took less than a class period to execute, but saved her much time because, as she put it, she understood where her students were more than ever before, which allowed her to teach more effectively. This process is just another example of a simple, yet effective way for teachers to accurately pre-assess where their students are and what they are ready for. Whether assessing students' knowledge of geography, scientific terms, literary devices, procedures in woodwork, or rules of a specific sport, we need to take the time to discover what knowledge students are bringing with them into any instructional context.

Accurate assessments, whether as pre-assessments or ongoing assessments throughout the learning process, provide important information that allows us to maximize the effectiveness of our instruction. Accurate information also allows students to self-assess and know their own status while there is still time to make corrections and improve. While identifying the *why, what,* and *how* of assessments is not the only way to build confident learners, it will go a long way in setting the stage for students to anticipate a positive result.

Tips for Communicating with Parents

- Clearly communicate to parents the purpose behind *formative* and *summative* assessments. Make sure that parents understand your learning and assessment goals. Once they know the purpose behind your processes and strategies, they can more effectively support their children.

- Clarify the learning targets so parents have a clear picture of what their children are supposed to learn and how it builds toward the big ideas and deeper understandings.

- Have students share the targets with their parents before the beginning of the unit, using student-friendly documents. Use these documents for student-led conferencing as a way of prompting students to explain what prior knowledge they had, where they needed extra support, and how they advanced through the learning.

- Encourage students to clearly identify for their parents the small steps necessary to achieve the bigger learning. In this way, parents will gain confidence in their ability to support their children through the learning process. They will also gain confidence in you and how you have logically sequenced the progression of ideas.

Guiding Questions for Individuals or Learning Teams

1. Is there a balanced assessment system in your class or do you favour one form of assessment (formative or summative) over the other? What would a *balanced* assessment system look like in your classroom?

2. Have you previously used student-friendly language in describing the intended learning outcomes of any lesson, unit, or subject? Describe how students (and parents) responded.

3. Reflect on your assessment methods. Do you over-rely on one particular format? Which method of assessment are you using the least?

4. How can assessment methods distort a student's true achievement or mastery?

5. Describe your experience with pre-assessments. What is the difference between a *pre-assessment* and a *pre-test*?

Suggested Readings for Further Study

- *Seven Strategies of Assessment for Learning* by Jan Chappuis

- *Making Classroom Assessment Work* by Anne Davies

- *Transformative Assessment* by James W. Popham

- *Ahead of the Curve: The Power of Assessment to Transform Teaching and Learning* by Douglas Reeves

- *Classroom Assessment for Student Learning: Doing It Right— Using It Well* by Richard Stiggins, Judith A. Arter, Jan Chappuis, and Stephen Chappuis

Chapter 4

Descriptive Feedback Matters

To be effective, feedback needs to cause thinking. Grades don't do that. Scores don't do that. And comments like "Good Job" don't do that either.

Dylan Wiliam

Teaching and learning, for the most part, is a social interaction between a teacher who knows or understands something and a student who doesn't. In schools, this relationship is obvious; however, the teacher–student relationship exists in many forms outside the school environment. Whether starting a new job, learning how to use a new piece of software, or understanding a new purchasing procedure, adults are also continually a part of the teacher–student dynamic. Continual interaction between teacher and student is necessary so that both clearly see the progress the student is making. This learning-focused interaction between teacher and student is where *descriptive feedback* can play a significant role: it allows students to know what they have done well and what steps they should take to grow.

Any kind of feedback is not enough. Students who grow and learn the most are the ones who are given descriptive feedback for the purpose of learning, not judgment. Descriptive feedback must come during the learning process and is most effective when students can use that feedback for corrective purposes. Given the number of students you may be responsible for teaching, descriptive feedback can present a challenge. However, without descriptive feedback, the classroom becomes a place where an adult disseminates information in hope that students can make sense of it and produce quality work without relevant feedback to support improvement.

Big Idea: Descriptive Feedback for Student Learning

Feedback in two general categories—*evaluative* and *descriptive*—will always occur in all classrooms.

Schools have always provided *evaluative* feedback. Giving this involves the teacher making a judgment about a student's level of progress at any given point during the instruction. Typically, the teacher examines the student's work and evaluates (judges) to what level the student has progressed. Subsequently, a grade or score is attached to the work and is reported to other people—parents, school board, and government—to verify the level of learning a student has attained.

Clearly, this type of feedback is quite prevalent in schools, is a necessary part of our school system, and will not be eliminated. However, these judgments are not focused on learning and do not provide students with any of the information needed to guide them to improve. Once a grade or a score is attached to a piece of work, students will likely believe that the work has been judged and the learning is complete.

The research on feedback is substantial and clear: effective feedback identifies both strengths and areas in need of corrective action. The research is also clear that once a grade or a score is attached to student work, the comments and feedback are rendered meaningless to most students, and the impact of descriptive feedback for the purpose of improvement is, at best, minimal (Butler, 1988). For many students, the existence of a grade is a signal that the learning event has been completed and no longer requires attention. While an interim score can be given in some instances, the most effective feedback *for* learning comes when no grade is attached to the work. Without a grade, students are more likely to focus on the comments and use them to improve the quality of their work. These comments constitute descriptive feedback.

Criteria for Quality Feedback

Beyond being descriptive, effective feedback, if it is to serve learning and improvement, must be timely, specific, understandable to the student, and usable on the student's part (Wiggins, 1998).

First, if descriptive feedback is not *timely*, it begins to lose its relevance. There is momentum to learning, but that momentum can be stalled if the feedback is not part of a regular and predictable routine established within the classroom. Whether students have done practice math questions or a science test, their learning is not being served if they have to wait a week or two before finding out what they did well and where they need to improve.

Second, quality feedback is *specific*. Comments such as "good job" or "this could be better" might represent feedback in the literal sense, but they don't help students understand the specific steps necessary for further learning. Assigning a letter or a score doesn't do that either. When a student gets a *C* without specific feedback, the student has no indication as to how the grade was constructed. The student might wonder: Was everything at an average level? Did I excel in some areas and fail at others? What action is necessary for my grade to improve? Grades, as discussed earlier, send a signal of finality to the students. If they are satisfied with their level of performance, the motivation to improve is diminished. "Good job" might make a student feel good, but it serves no purpose in describing what the student did well and what requires corrective action.

One challenge with descriptive feedback, especially if it comes via a rubric, leads us to the third aspect of quality feedback. Too often, descriptive feedback is written in *teacher-friendly* language that is not accessible to most students or parents. Beyond needing to be timely and specific, descriptive feedback needs to be *understandable* to the receiver. For many students, especially our most challenged learners, descriptive feedback and the language of a rubric can be lost in translation. *"The conclusion is strong and leaves the reader solidly understanding your position. Effective restatement of the position statement begins the closing paragraph."* When faced with such specific feedback, students can be left feeling overwhelmed because they don't understand what the comment means and, therefore, have no idea what to do in response.

For this reason, teachers should use student-friendly rubrics and scoring guides. They should also teach the specific criteria found within a rubric ahead of time by using examples of strong and weak work. Students will become more comfortable with the descriptions and more likely to act upon feedback. Figure 4.1 (see next page) shows two rubric portions with student-friendly translations immediately below. While we might want students to understand the traditional criteria statements, using the student-friendly language removes a potential barrier for some students who, while working independently, might find it difficult to decipher what to do next.

No matter how student friendly a rubric is, there will have to be some instruction on the criteria statements. After all, even the most student-friendly rubrics are still written using semi-formal language. A student-friendly rubric can still be academic and use age-appropriate vocabulary. The key is to make sure that the specific statements within the rubric are written in a way that students, when working independently, will clearly understand. The sooner students can internalize the expectations, the more likely they are to reflect them in their own work. McTighe and O'Connor (2005) recommend we ask ourselves one simple question about our feedback systems: *Can learners tell specifically from given feedback what they have done well and what they could do next time to improve?* If the answer is "no," then clearly our feedback needs to be more specific and presented in a way that makes sense to the students.

Any descriptive feedback that students can't act upon is useless feedback. This observation leads us to the fourth aspect of quality feedback identified by Wiggins—*the opportunity to act*. It is rare that anyone produces a perfect assignment or completes a task perfectly on a first attempt. More typical is making a concerted first effort, understanding what was strong and weak about that first

Figure 4.1: Sample Student-Friendly Rubric—Persuasive Essay

Category	Not Yet	Approaching	Meets	Exceeds
Position Statement	There is no position statement present.	A position statement is present, but it does not make your position clear.	The position statement provides a clear statement of your position on the topic.	The position statement provides a clear, strong statement of your position on the topic.
Student-Friendly Position	*You haven't told the reader the opinion you have about your topic.*	*You have given the reader an opinion, but it isn't really clear.*	*You have told the reader the opinion you are taking on your topic.*	*You have made your opinion of your topic clear and strong.*
Transitions	Transitions between ideas are unclear or non-existent.	Some transitions work well, but some connections between ideas are not clear.	Transitions show how ideas are connected, but there is little variety.	A variety of thoughtful transitions are used. They clearly show how ideas are connected.
Student-Friendly Position	*There is no connection between your ideas.*	*There are some vague connections between your ideas, but they are not obvious.*	*The connections between your ideas are obvious, but you present them in the same way every time.*	*Connections between your ideas are not only obvious, but you have shown them in a few different ways.*

effort, and then making a second attempt. That attempt–feedback cycle is, again, the core of the instructional process:

> The feedback on tests, seatwork, and homework should give each pupil guidance on how to improve, and each pupil must be given help and an opportunity to work on the improvement. (Black & Wiliam, 1998, p. 144)

The opportunity to act is, in many ways, our first filter for descriptive feedback. If we do not plan on giving students the help and time needed to improve, then the timeliness, specificity, and clarity of our feedback is irrelevant. If we are to maximize our students' readiness to meet learning outcomes during summative events, then enabling them to act on descriptive feedback derived from formative assessment must be our priority.

Putting It into Practice

Teaching is coaching and so feedback needs to be constructive and specific.

All feedback, whether descriptive or evaluative, must avoid comparisons between students. The comparison is to the learning targets, outcomes, or specific criteria, not to the performance levels reached by the other students. Those who have, for example, coached a sports team or directed a drama production understand the power of descriptive feedback and the impact it can have on performances. Descriptive feedback focuses on learning, on improvement, and on corrections.

Teachers often use the most descriptive feedback for the performance-based subjects with specific criteria, such as physical education, art, woodwork, and drama. For some reason, when teachers are put into a coaching situation, the need and use of descriptive feedback seems to be more obvious. If we were to teach like we coach, our classrooms would be transformed into interactive centres for improvement and quality, focused on building confidence through the identification of both strengths and weaknesses.

Providing Feedback That Builds Confidence

Let us apply the coaching metaphor to the classroom. The coach (teacher) has the vision of what success looks like. Whether it is the overall team performance or individual performance, the coach knows what to look for in each athlete and the kind of corrective action necessary—the coach is the expert. All through the season there are *summative* checkpoints of quality (competition with other teams) and periods where *formative* corrective action is possible (practices). The coach makes strategic use of the periods to promote development.

Imagine coaching a team that was performing poorly at the beginning of the season. Would you ever tell team members that you've given them the opportunity to play, and if they choose to go out and lose week after week, that's their problem? Unfortunately, while that scenario is highly unlikely, some teachers have created that condition within the classroom: students are getting an opportunity to learn, and if they choose to fail, it's their problem.

Effective coaches analyze their team's performance to determine what they are doing well and what they need to work on. The team then practises what needs to be improved to increase overall performance quality. Coaches, after a poor team performance, would not simply tell their team that they need to get better, need to get their act together, or need to work harder, without giving specifics as to *what* they need to get better at, what *act* they need to get together, or on *what* aspect they need to work harder. Neither should teachers.

Effective coaches have several qualities in common:

- **They motivate their players.** They understand their individual athletes and what motivates them to be their best. Some require toughness, while others require a more gentle approach. Either way, effective coaches tailor their feedback according to what they know about their individual players.

- **They remain positive.** They continually have faith in their team, believe they can improve, and believe that, as coaches, they have the answers to how that improvement or quality performance can manifest.

- **They inspire their team and nurture their confidence.**
  Effective coaches believe that their team can succeed even when their players don't think they can.

If we taught like we coached, our students would experience the same inspiration, the same motivation, and the same levels of increased confidence. Ultimately, the players have to take responsibility and ownership for the successes or failures of the team since the coach can do everything but play the game (see Chapter 6 on ownership); however, right up until performance (summative assessments), coaches can have a major influence on how ready their players are to compete.

Describing Both Challenges and Strengths

Having taught both English and social studies at several grade levels, I have graded my fair share of essays. Early in my career, I was the classic example of a teacher who "did what was done to him" in terms of assessing and providing feedback. I was far too focused on the mechanics of writing and not focused enough on the ideas presented within the writing. As time went on, I realized that students' writing was not improving because I wasn't giving the students the opportunity to improve it. No published author writes a best-selling novel on the first attempt. Edits, rewrites, and revisions are all part of the writing process, yet here I as a teacher was expecting 15-year-old students to get it right the first time.

At that moment, I began to question the writing process I was putting my students through. I had to decide how to best improve writing and whether I was giving my students the best chance to succeed. I had to decide whether students should write six essays once or three essays twice. With no extra minutes available in the school day or semester, I had to make a judgment on how best to improve student performance.

Ultimately, I wanted my students to learn how to write to the best of their ability; however, I concluded that my current practice was too focused on writing production. A task completion–focused exercise in producing essays gave the appearance of rigour, but marginalized the opportunities to grow. I decided to reduce the number of essays my students had to write but allow them to use my feedback to improve their essays. The feedback I was giving was their opportunity to make the necessary improvements and demonstrate that they had learned how to improve the quality of their writing. I became more focused on learning.

I have learned two important lessons since I began using descriptive feedback.

The first is that the *quality* of the feedback is more important than the existence of descriptive feedback. As I gained experience with descriptive feedback, I realized that the students' ability to use my feedback was dependent on the quality of the feedback I provided. Quality feedback describes both strengths and challenges. Early on, I was more focused on a deficit model, identifying only what was wrong. While areas of improvement are important, it is equally important to balance the feedback by identifying strengths. This essential goes back to confidence: students need to know that some things about their work are effective and good, and that other things need to improve. Once I began identifying strengths, student motivation to use the feedback increased.

Determining Student Readiness for Feedback

The second lesson I learned was that my descriptive feedback had to be tailored to what students were ready for and what they could realistically act upon. While quality is important, finding the right balance with the amount of feedback students receive is also critical. As my own capacity grew, I began to provide feedback only to the level at which students would feel confident they could use the feedback to improve their work. I gave the students who were more proficient writers more complex feedback, while I provided the students who were less proficient with more fundamental feedback. This approach is not about lowering standards; it's more about taking strategic consideration of what each individual student can handle.

Remember, feedback that students can't act upon is useless feedback, so while I might be able to provide the same, high-level descriptive feedback to all students, not all of them are at a point where they can act upon that feedback equally. If a student struggles with essay structure and has not used five distinct paragraphs, giving that student feedback on *how to make an argument more coherent* or *how to use a more inviting voice within the writing* might not be as critical. This perspective speaks to differentiating our feedback to put all of our students in a position to improve (see Chapter 5 for information on differentiation). Feedback that sits far beyond a student's ability is more discouraging than helpful. Descriptive feedback, if serving its true purpose, will comfortably put students in a position to improve the quality of their work.

Using Rubrics for Focus

Strength-based, learning-focused descriptive feedback looks, sounds, and feels different than the assignment of a grade. Here is an example: *"Your ideas are well organized into five well-developed paragraphs and use effective transitions between each. However, your ideas lose focus and some of the examples don't directly support the topic sentences of your body paragraphs. While your sentence structure is generally good, there are some grammar conventions that interfere with the clarity of your argument."* With that kind of feedback, the student has a clear picture of what is good, what needs work, and how his or her writing can improve for the next attempt or new assignment.

In thinking about the previous example, it is easy to see why providing descriptive feedback can be a daunting task for teachers. Imagine teaching three or four sections of the same English class, and having to provide descriptive feedback on 90 to 120 papers—the thought alone is exhausting. For this reason, the use of rubrics has become more prevalent. Rubrics are simply a tool, while the criteria established within the tool provide the descriptive feedback. The rubric is a way of organizing the descriptive feedback in a way that makes sense to everyone involved.

Figure 4.2 (see next page) provides an example of how to organize a typical rubric. Rubrics are not new; however, the way in which we use rubrics is somewhat new. While nothing can replace personal comments specific to an individual learner's needs, the rubric provides a baseline from which to assess the quality of the work and to provide students with descriptive feedback on the quality that their work represents.

Figure 4.2: Sample Rubric—Persuasive Essay

Category	Not Yet	Approaching	Meets	Exceeds
Position Statement	There is no position statement present.	A position statement is present, but it does not make your position clear.	The position statement provides a clear statement of your position on the topic.	The position statement provides a clear, strong statement of your position on the topic.
Thesis Statement	The thesis statement does not name the topic and does not preview what will be discussed.	The thesis statement outlines some or all of the main points to be discussed but does not name the topic.	The thesis statement names the topic of the essay.	The thesis statement names the topic for the essay and outlines the main points to be discussed.
Transitions	Transitions between ideas are unclear or non-existent.	Some transitions work well, but some connections between ideas are not clear.	Transitions show how ideas are connected, but there is little variety.	A variety of thoughtful transitions are used. They clearly show how ideas are connected.

■ ■ ■

Figure 4.2 (continued)

Category	Not Yet	Approaching	Meets	Exceeds
Closing Paragraph	There is no conclusion —the paper just ends.	Your position is restated within the closing paragraph, but not near the beginning.	The conclusion is recognizable. Your position is restated within the first two sentences of the closing paragraph.	The conclusion is strong and leaves the reader solidly understanding your position. Effective restatement of the position statement begins the closing paragraph.
Sentence Structure	Most sentences are not well constructed or varied.	Most sentences are well constructed, but there is no variation in structure.	Most sentences are well constructed, and there is some variety in how the sentences are constructed.	All sentences are well constructed with varied structure.

Rubrics are an effective way to assess performance and product targets for three reasons:

1. A rubric identifies the standard, or outcome, that the student is expected to strive toward, usually in the far right-hand column. Students then know what the standard of quality is even when they are working independently.

2. The criteria set within a rubric address specific aspects of quality. In the sample rubric shown in Figure 4.2, each category identifies several specific aspects of quality writing and the specific description of what those categories look like at each level. The rubric makes it clear to students which aspects of the assignment are most important; it ensures they are not distracted by unimportant aspects of quality, such as the number of colours used on a poster or the number of words in a paragraph.

3. A rubric effectively identifies the path students should take to improve. It shows students what they are proficient at and what they need to improve. Students can compare their level of quality with the level of quality expected. In between where they are and where they need to be is the path to improvement.

For teachers, the differentiated instruction comes in teaching students how to move themselves along their own learning continuum (see Chapter 5). For students, their ability to work independently and take ownership increases as they have a guideline that will keep them focused on the important details of quality work (see Chapter 6).

Co-constructing the rubric criteria is an excellent way to involve students right from the beginning of the assignment. Co-constructing builds ownership and deepens student understanding of what quality work looks like. Our job is to make sure that the foundation is set to maximize the benefits of co-constructing criteria. Student-friendly learning targets allow students to know what the focus should be. If the learning targets are clear, then students will be less easily distracted by colour, font size, and special effects that may add a little extra to the work, but are not critical to meeting the assignment's criteria. One of our roles is to keep students focused on the targets so they can avoid those distractions.

Addressing the Time Factor

Evaluative feedback is, quite simply, more efficient than descriptive feedback; however, descriptive feedback is more effective. Teachers often worry about finding enough time to provide descriptive feedback to a class of diverse learners. Indeed, it is not possible for a teacher to provide *all* of the descriptive feedback to *all* of the students on *all* of their assignments, including *all* of the specific aspects of quality. Teachers who have had the most success with descriptive feedback find that it is possible only once students are engaged in self- and peer-assessment.

While we will discuss student involvement in the assessment process in Chapter 6, take note that teaching students how to provide descriptive feedback to themselves and others gives you flexibility and choice on where to spend the most time. One possibility is to focus feedback on one specific element you want to ensure that all students have mastered. Another is to focus your efforts on the most vulnerable learners. Still another is to focus only on the feedback that was missed during peer assessment. The point is that flexibility and choice are options only once students play a role in the feedback process.

Save your judgments in the form of grades or scores for the end of the learning process. Descriptive feedback serves its purpose during the learning, when there is still time for students to make changes, improve their status, and be better prepared. The reality of school is that summative assessments are necessary to verify that learning has occurred and to produce grades and scores that report how students are progressing. Mixing descriptive feedback and summative assessments is not necessary. At the end of the learning cycle, descriptive feedback is unnecessary; during the learning cycle, it is most crucial.

Tips for Communicating with Parents

- Let parents know your intent when providing descriptive feedback without a grade or score. As parents see that your focus is on describing the next steps in the learning process, they will feel more comfortable with the absence of a score.

- Educate parents that during the learning process, it is not the time for a score or a grade. Instead, your focus is on maximizing their child's learning in preparation for the graded assignment or event.

- When parents ask you how their child is doing, describe all of the student's strengths and challenges without the use of a grade. When parents ask what their child's grade is, tell them you don't know yet as they haven't finished all of the necessary learning for you to make an accurate judgment.

- Make the feedback you provide to students accessible to parents as well. Doing this will help manage any potential negative emotional responses to what is being assigned.

- Parents may become frustrated when their child is asked to improve a piece of work in a way that is far beyond the child's level. Make sure parents know that the feedback you provide will always put the students on the edge of improvement.

Guiding Questions for Individuals or Learning Teams

1. Think of a time when you tried to learn something new, but quit as a result of your lack of progress. Was someone teaching you? Was the feedback more evaluative or descriptive while you were learning? Did the kind of feedback play a role in why you quit learning?

2. Of the four aspects of quality feedback described in this chapter—*timely, specific, understandable,* and *usable*—which one are you currently MOST effective at providing? How have you sustained that over time?

3. Of the four aspects of quality feedback described in this chapter—*timely, specific, understandable,* and *usable*—which one are you currently LEAST effective at providing? What do you think it will take for you to improve in this area?

4. Why is making use of descriptive feedback easier in a coaching situation than in a teaching situation? How can we bring more coaching to our classrooms? What would need to change to do this?

5. How often are students permitted to act upon the feedback you provide on the quality of their work?

6. Do you have any experience co-constructing criteria with students? From your experience, what are the biggest benefits and challenges to this process?

7. How will you find or make the time to provide more descriptive feedback to students?

Suggested Readings for Further Study

- *Feedback for Learning* edited by Susan Askew

- *How to Give Effective Feedback to Your Students* by Susan M. Brookhart

- *Seven Strategies of Assessment for Learning* by Jan Chappuis

- "The Power of Feedback" by John Hattie and Helen Timperley in *Review of Educational Research*

- *Classroom Assessment for Student Learning: Doing It Right—Using It Well* by Richard Stiggins, Judith A. Arter, Jan Chappuis, and Stephen Chappuis

Chapter 5

Differentiated Instruction Matters

> *Ultimately, just one question might best serve diverse learners, their teachers, and their society. What can we do to support educators in developing the skill and the will to teach for each learner's equity of access to excellence?*
>
> **Carol Ann Tomlinson**

Differentiated instruction must occur if students are to close the gap between where they are now and where they are going. The instructional process and framework bridge the assessments *for* learning and the assessments *of* learning. With learning being developmental and individualized, it makes sense that the instruction each student receives is differentiated to his or her needs.

We are currently at a crossroads in education where the *scope-and-sequence* and the *assessment for learning* paradigms exist in an obvious paradox. A scope-and-sequence sets out a detailed plan of action for a course or an individual unit of study within that course. By doing so, instructional decisions within a scope-and-sequence are made by the teacher, independent of any information gathered about the individual learners enrolled in that class. Often, these decisions are made in the summer and are recycled (with minor adjustments) year after year.

On the other hand, as we've discussed in previous chapters, many teachers are now using assessments *for* learning to gather information about students' levels of proficiency to decide the next steps of instruction—something that can't be done in the summer. While it is possible to scope-and-sequence once a pre-assessment has been completed, in the traditional sense, the scope-and sequence is losing its relevance in today's educational world. The bottom line is that if we forge ahead and teach *what* and *how* we've always taught, we will likely over-teach skills and content the students have already mastered and under-teach other skills and topics some students need extra time with. Differentiating our instruction will allow us to take that final step to fulfilling our mission: educating all students to at least a minimal proficiency.

Differentiated instruction is the only way we can meet the needs of all learners. Many of us, though, are already differentiating our instruction without realizing it. It is important to recognize this, as it will add a level of comfort to a process and mindset that may feel foreign and awkward. Once we realize we are already differentiating in even a small way, we will quickly see that the approach is not so intimidating. We will then feel comfortable expanding our repertoire to create more differentiated opportunities for our students.

Big Idea: Formative Assessment Leads to Differentiated Instruction

If the goal is to cover the prescribed curriculum in a predetermined sequence using a narrow set of instructional strategies regardless of how students learn, what motivates them, or what they are ready for, then differentiated instruction is *not* something that teachers would consider. Carol Ann Tomlinson, widely considered as the leading expert on the subject, defines differentiation as "student-aware teaching." She believes that the goal of differentiation is to maximize student potential by helping students grow as much and as rapidly as possible (Tomlinson, 2008). Maximizing success, she argues, is possible only when we are aware of each student's strengths, areas in need of improvement, ways of learning most effectively, special interest in the topic at hand, and instructional readiness.

Underpinnings of Differentiation

Before we even entertain the idea of differentiation, some prerequisites need to be met. Having the prerequisites in place will make differentiation possible and maximize its impact.

1. **Develop student-friendly learning targets to make the intended learning clear and accessible** (see Chapter 3). The impact of differentiation is maximized when the specific learning targets are identified throughout the process.

2. **Get to know the students at a more intimate level.** For many teachers, especially high-school teachers, this task is challenging. While getting to know everything about each student on a personal level may not be possible, it is important to at least understand what motivates students, how they learn, and what they are ready for, so we can make the curriculum more relevant to the individual student.

3. **Commit to continuous monitoring of student progress.** As students learn, grow, and improve, new motivation and readiness will evolve. Without this continuous monitoring (assessment *for* learning), teachers will likely lose sight of where students are along their own learning continuum; mismatched instructional methods and an inefficient use of instructional time could result.

4. **Accurately assess for learning information.** Without accurate assessment for learning information, appropriate differentiation is next to impossible. Using assessment for learning strategies to continuously monitor students gives us information about when, where, why, and how to differentiate.

Guiding Principles of Differentiation

Differentiation is a mindset, not an event or a prescription for teaching. I can't emphasize this idea enough. Having a differentiated mindset is more critical than using specific tools or strategies. Differentiation can occur before, during, and after instruction.

Typically, opportunities to differentiate present themselves at different times during lessons and assignments. In some ways, we can consider differentiation as something we can do at various points of entry during the whole learning process. According to Tomlinson, as teachers respond to the needs of the learners, differentiation is guided by three general principles.

1. **Respectful Tasks:** Respectful tasks keep every student at the edge of improvement, are focused on the essential knowledge, skills, and understandings of the lesson, and allow students to think at their highest level possible. Respectful tasks increase motivation by allowing students to find their work interesting and powerful, as well as respecting students as equal partners in the learning process. We must appreciate where every student is in his or her learning and honour it through meaningful, thoughtful, and respectful tasks.

2. **Flexible Groupings:** One misunderstanding about differentiation is that students always work alone. Effective teachers know that learning is maximized when there is a balance between individual, small-group, and whole-class learning. By using flexible groupings, we can avoid creating a learning environment where students view themselves or others in a narrow, limited way. If only one or two types of groupings are used, students can miss out on interacting with most of their classmates.

3. **Continual Assessment:** Everything a student says or does is a potential source of assessment data. While assessments should be ongoing and flexible, there should also be distinct stages that allow for structured adjustments by teachers. While the minute-by-minute formative moments allow us to make minor adjustments throughout a lesson, the more structured assessments provide us with the opportunity to make more significant enhancements to the instructional plan. These assessments, according to Tomlinson, should maximize the opportunity for each student to open the widest possible window on his or her learning.

The biggest idea is to know where students are in their learning and through differentiation to keep each student on the edge of improvement as much as possible. By using the guiding principles of respectful tasks, flexible groupings, and continual assessments, we will create a learning environment ready for differentiated lessons that meet the needs of all students, during every lesson, throughout every day.

Putting It into Practice

Teachers need to get past five myths about differentiated instruction before they can adopt the differentiation mindset in their classrooms.

Before identifying what differentiated instruction is and what it might look like within a classroom, it is important to know what it is not and what it doesn't look like. Common misunderstandings can lead to a false sense that differentiation is not possible, is an overwhelming prospect, and is something that the average teacher can't attain.

Myth #1: Differentiated instruction is about creating individual lesson plans.

The idea that a teacher has the time or the energy to create individualized lesson plans for every student in the class is both unrealistic and absurd. This notion of individual lesson plans might be the biggest misconception of differentiated instruction. While there are times when a teacher might provide individualized instruction to a student to move the young person's learning forward, individualized lesson plans have never been promoted as a goal of differentiated instruction.

Myth #2: Differentiated instruction does not allow teachers to "teach."

This myth suggests that teachers will never be able to *deliver* instruction, since all of the students will be working at their own pace so will not be at the same point when whole-class presentation is needed. Differentiated instruction is not only about individual and small-group work. Effective instruction incorporates a host of methods, including whole-class instruction. Whole-class presentation is an integral part of every classroom. Individual and small-group work cannot match the teacher's ability to model, provide direction, share experiences, and create excitement for learning. Finding a balance of methods and using them at the appropriate time is what effective teaching and learning is all about.

Myth #3: Differentiated instruction makes the more capable students work harder.

Differentiated instruction is not about creating an unbalanced or unfair workload. By doing this, we could create classrooms filled with animosity and reduced motivation. This type of classroom would breed mediocrity as students would slow down their learning to manage their workloads. While allowing students more time to complete an assignment can be an appropriate response, it is not a cornerstone of differentiation. Fairness is evident when each student is struggling appropriately. Effective teaching occurs when each student is struggling enough to learn something new (Morreale, 2000). The goal is to put students in situations where they consistently sit on the edge of improvement—they don't know the answer—as often as possible.

Myth #4: Differentiated instruction is designed for students with special learning needs.

Differentiated instruction is not the same as adapting or modifying the curriculum. It is also not a method of remediation designed only for students with learning disabilities. Rather, adaptations and modifications are an integral part of the educational programming for students with special needs. Differentiated instruction can be more inclusive, as it takes into account a student's learning needs, style, and motivation; however, it is not exclusive to a select group of students. Gifted learners will benefit from a classroom using differentiated instruction strategies as much as students with learning challenges will. It is *how* we teach and the mindset we use when creating learning opportunities, not simply *what* we do when students don't learn the first time.

Myth #5: Differentiated instruction is the magic answer.
Being an effective teacher is challenging and complex, and while it is natural to search for that one strategy or idea that will alleviate all of our concerns, that strategy doesn't exist. We are not one differentiated strategy away from educational utopia. Differentiated instruction is part of an effective teacher's repertoire to be used at the right time and place within the learning continuum. Differentiated instruction has proven to be effective, but by making it more than it is, we overstate its applicability and overpromise its impact.

Determining What Can Be Differentiated

Prior to instruction, we consider what the students, both individually and as a group, are ready for. Part of differentiated instruction is considering whether or not students are ready for the next topic of study. If student motivation to learn a topic might be a problem, then we could consider creating a lesson plan that includes some option of choice. While the curriculum itself may not be optional, allowing students a choice within the curriculum can control for motivation. It is rarely necessary that all students read the same book, produce the same project, or learn in the same manner. Allowing some choices not only increases student interest, but also empowers them during the learning. In addition, while planning, we would also consider how students learn and whether the lesson style is a good fit for their learning styles. In cases where the fit is poor, we must have a plan to follow up with students for whom the lesson was not a fit. An example of this might be having some visual material ready for students who find lecture-style lessons least effective. In any event, an important aspect of differentiated instruction is to keep learning styles and preferences in mind while planning.

The differentiated mindset is really one where teachers consider all aspects of the lesson and decide whether differentiation is necessary to maximize student success. We can differentiate for lesson content, process, product, or environment (Tomlinson, 2003). We need not differentiate every aspect of every lesson; rather, we can look for opportunities to personalize the learning experience for each student in the class. Throughout every lesson, there are always some things that are non-negotiable, that simply must be the same for every student. When that is the case, we can differentiate for other aspects of the lesson to personalize the experience for students. The intent, as always, is to differentiate for student readiness, interest, or learning profile.

Below are some questions and suggestions on how to work around the aspect of learning that every student must complete.

1. **What if specific *content* has to be covered?**

   If the content of instruction (e.g., the causes of World War I, photosynthesis, or literary devices) is non-negotiable, differentiate   process by which the students learn the content, the products they produce as a result of learning, or the environment (e.g., location or groupings) in which they learn.

2. **What if the *process* of learning has to be followed?**

   If the process of instruction (e.g., a science experiment, shooting of a basketball, or a persuasive essay) is non-negotiable, differentiate for the content, the end product, or the learning environment. While students might be required to write a persuasive essay, students could determine the content of that essay, which allows for choice and differentiates for interest and motivation. Simply put, students are more likely to write an essay when the topic interests them.

3. **What if the *product* is non-negotiable?**

   Few products are non-negotiable. Students do have to, for example, produce essays or lab reports, but again, other aspects of the lesson can be differentiated. What the students write about or the type of experiment they conduct can be differentiated to fit their interests, learning styles, or readiness.

4. **What if the *learning environment* is non-negotiable?**
   By now the pattern should be self-evident. If students, for example, must work alone, then all other aspects of the lesson can be differentiated. There is also the reality that most learning occurs within the same classroom; however, groupings, partnerships, or cooperative activities (such as think-pair-share or jigsaws) can add the needed differentiation to increase student engagement.

Not everything in every lesson can (or should) be differentiated. The differentiated instruction mindset is about teachers looking for opportunities to differentiate outside of the non-negotiable parts found within every lesson, section, or unit of study. Some topics *have* to be covered, some processes *have* to be followed, some products *have* to be produced, and some environments *have* to be the same. All or nothing is not the answer. By differentiating when the opportunities present to maximize the effectiveness of each lesson, we will truly meet the learning needs of all students.

Getting Started with Differentiation

Like almost every aspect of teaching, we learn more from *doing* than from just *knowing*. Getting started is the most important aspect of differentiation; however, there are some important things to keep in mind as we move forward with differentiating our classrooms. While differentiation is not overly complex, it does take some practice to recognize where differentiation can maximize student success and at which *point of entry* differentiation will be most effective.

Most teachers already differentiate in one way or another, even if they don't realize they are doing it. Examine your current practice and find places where choice and opportunity are already an option—begin to expand from there. Our collective efforts in literacy, especially over the past decade, make it the most obvious place where differentiated instruction occurs. The class novel has been replaced with students choosing books of high interest and at an appropriate reading level. Literature circles provide the opportunity for flexible groupings and differentiated content. Chances are differentiation is already happening within most classrooms; examine where and move forward from there, as this is likely the area where you are most comfortable beginning.

While I was at McNicoll Park Middle School (2003–06), we began to develop a school-wide literacy program that made some fundamental shifts toward more appropriate literacy instruction. We focused on developing a process, lessons, assessment tools, and timelines around the reading strategies we were teaching our students. Our work supported all teachers in moving forward on our ever-emerging literacy goal of developing a minimal proficiency in all students.

Figure 5.1 (see next page) is one simple example of a tool that our team developed. While the tool is not overly complicated, use of the tool is where differentiating can occur. Our approach to literacy instruction, like most schools at the time, shifted appropriately to having students read books they were interested in and ready for—two of the three guiding principles behind differentiation. We didn't call it "differentiation" at the time, but looking back, that's exactly what we were doing. Figure 5.1 is an example of a tool meant to give students practice in drawing inferences, using prior knowledge, and asking questions. At its bottom is part of a student-friendly rubric that describes for students the various levels of proficiency within each skill or strategy. We used this rubric to allow students to self-assess their own reading skills and know what successful growth would look like.

Here is where the differentiation comes in. Two teachers in our school, Steve DeVito (Grade 8) and Darcy Mullin (Grade 7), used all of the activities and tools we developed in a differentiated manner when they altered their routines around silent reading. One cornerstone of any literacy program is that the students have more time to read. The challenge with silent reading is that some students read and others fake-read. Steve and Darcy wanted to create an *active* silent reading time where students were reading, but were also striving to improve in an area that needed some focus and attention.

We had various activities for the various strategies. While silent reading was taking place, students would have the tool that

Building from Clues

(Activate prior knowledge, draw inferences, ask questions.)

Where?	**When?**
Who?	**What?**

Using the activity above, can you make any conclusions about the passage/
selection you have read today? If yes, explain clearly. If no, discuss when
this activity might be useful. _____

_____

_____

_____

_____

■ ■ ■

Figure 5.1 (continued)

Can you make any comparisons to when something similar happened, either in real life or in another story? _____

_____

_____

_____

_____

Strategies	Not Yet	Meeting	Exceeding
Drawing Inferences During and After Reading	❏ I can't generate meaning from the clues in the text. ❏ I am not able to identify and use clues in the text to "read between the lines" to identify theme, character traits, and/or motivation. ❏ I am not able to use evidence from the text to support my inferences and/or make connections.	❏ I can generate meaning when the clues in the text are obvious. ❏ I am able to identify and use clues in the text to "read between the lines" to identify theme, character traits, and/or motivation, except when the text is difficult or unfamiliar. ❏ I sometimes find it difficult to use evidence from the text to support my inferences and/or make connections.	❏ I can generate meaning even when the clues in the text are less obvious. ❏ I am able to identify and use clues in the text to "read between the lines" to identify theme, character traits, and/or motivation. ❏ I use evidence from the text to support my inferences and/or make connections.

corresponded with the strategy they were working on. In the case of Figure 5.1, students would read a book appropriate for them, then answer the questions and focus on their ability to make inferences. Active silent reading required students to do more than read different books; they also had to complete different activities based on their needs. While one student might be working on drawing inferences, other students could be working on synthesizing information, using prior knowledge, extracting main idea, or building vocabulary. Active silent reading really was differentiating based upon student interest and readiness.

Naryn Searcy, a teacher at Princess Margaret Secondary School in Penticton, British Columbia, uses a differentiated approach during the learning process by giving her Grade 12 students options for how they might show-what-they-know about any pieces of literature the class is analyzing. These options are given frequently throughout a semester and allow students to choose how they might express the full depth and breadth of their learning. Students are given permission to use written, verbal, artistic, dramatic, or musical means of expression. The options are limitless and restricted only by the students' own imagination and creativity. Students often work in groups—groups that tend to be made up of individuals who gravitate toward the use of the same medium. Outgoing students tend to choose a skit or dramatization option; artistic students choose drawing. The goal is to differentiate for student strengths and talents by removing the *medium* as a barrier. Naryn provides the students with a checklist or rubric of what learning outcomes the students' demonstrations must fulfill. She believes it's essential to do this to keep students focused on *why* they are creating their demonstrations through their chosen medium.

When other teachers first hear of what Naryn's students are permitted to do, many immediately reject the idea because they don't feel they could assess a piece of art, lyrics to a song, a puppet show, or a dramatization. This response completely misses the point. Naryn doesn't evaluate the art, the lyrics, or the dramatization—she assesses the learning outcomes for English Literature.

A teacher doesn't have to know how to evaluate a painting or a song, she says. A teacher need only recognize the intended learning outcomes for his or her particular course. Factors such as creativity, artistic ability, or effort are not being assessed; therefore, the same checklist or rubric can be used to assess the work regardless of the method the students use. The *learning* is the end; the *medium of expression* is the means. For Naryn, it doesn't matter how nice the puppets look or how clearly students project their voices during a skit; what matters is whether students can demonstrate an understanding of the key elements of the poem, short story, or novel in question.

Another surprise for many teachers is that these projects often don't "count." In other words, there is no score that will eventually contribute to a report card grade. Although effort is not assessed, students typically put forth the kind of effort most teachers would envy. Because the students choose the medium, the project doesn't *feel* like work. The individual summative assessments come later.

The projects are an opportunity for students to use a medium they prefer to demonstrate how much they have learned throughout the course of study. If an element is missing, Naryn highlights that element and follows up with the individual or group to ensure that any gaps are filled. To increase individual accountability, at times Naryn asks students one at a time to verbally demonstrate their understanding at the end of the completed project.

For senior English Literature classes, Naryn's classes are surprisingly heterogeneous in composition. Her classes consist of gifted students, students with learning disabilities, and students who demonstrate challenging behaviours. All students who enroll in Naryn's class know they will be given the maximum opportunity to succeed because they will be allowed to learn in their own way through their own medium. Much of the content is non-negotiable; however, the means by which students can demonstrate the learning is not. The permission to choose a method the students favour increases their confidence from the start. The commitment to completing the projects is unwavering, and the outcomes typically exceed expectations.

Differentiating Without Compromise

Most teachers I've worked with would say that differentiating instruction is not as complex as it appears. For most, the myths of differentiation seem to be more of an issue than the differentiating process itself. As noted earlier, some things can't be differentiated; however, there are many opportunities for teachers to differentiate within each lesson.

The challenge, which gets easier through practice, is to look for the opportunities to differentiate without compromising the integrity of the assignment. By following the simple guidelines below, teachers will gain the confidence and insight necessary to further differentiate their students' learning experiences and deepen their own understanding of how differentiation can be infused into their everyday classroom practice.

Start small; start slow. Like any other change or improvement, it is important to have a goal in mind, but to take small steps toward that goal. By taking small steps, teachers will ensure that differentiation becomes a new habit. If teachers try to differentiate too much too soon, they risk being overwhelmed and reverting back to old habits. Begin with one aspect of differentiation. Do what is most comfortable, and then expand from there.

Know your students. Take the time to get to know your students. If teachers are going to differentiate for interest, readiness, or learning style, knowing their students at a more intimate level is important. Remember, differentiation is for *all* students but is most effective for our most vulnerable learners. So, if you must prioritize, then know your vulnerable learners intimately to maximize the impact differentiation has for them. Previous teachers and report cards can provide some insight, but be sure to use pre-assessments or conferences with them to find out what interests them, how they like to learn, and what they are ready for.

Keep your standards high. Teachers should not lower their standards for individual learners. Expecting less from some students is not differentiation. When in doubt, teach "up." While some students will likely need extra support and guidance along the way, we need to convey to students that everyone is capable if given the appropriate opportunity. While raising the expectations for all students is most effective, expecting all of the students to produce at a high level without teacher intervention to various degrees is not. When students don't reach the expected levels of achievement, they need to be met with high levels of support rather than an increasing use of punitive consequences. All students can learn, and while they might not learn at the pace we'd like them to, we need to support their individual achievement and growth.

Remember, it's not about more. Differentiation means different, not more. Allowing some students to answer 10 questions while the more capable students answer 20 is an example of adaptation, not differentiation. If the more capable students are always expected to do more, then the incentive to excel could be diminished in some students. Similarly, students will question why they are trying so hard if the result is additional and, potentially, more difficult work. As educators, we see the value of more difficult work, but the students likely won't. Differentiation means we are headed to the same destination, and while we might take different routes to get there, we will all get there.

Most teachers respond favourably once they realize that differentiating a lesson is easier than first thought. Indeed, once we realize how we are already differentiating, intimidation gives way to excitement about the fact that meeting the needs of all learners is possible. If we can give up the auto-pilot nature of some of our practices and realize that there are simple, yet effective ways to lead students to the same learning outcomes via different paths, our instruction will have a renewed relevance and connectedness to the students we teach.

Recognizing the Affect of Differentiation

While differentiation serves a cognitive purpose, affective dimensions are equally important to the students' success. Differentiated classrooms become strength-based learning environments that allow students to engage in learning situations where they have some proficiency. That is not to say we ignore weaknesses; rather, we take full advantage of what students do well to keep them confident and energize their learning. Improvement, as we will explore further in Chapter 9, is important; however, to expect all weaknesses to be eliminated goes too far. The strength-based aspect of differentiation will likely produce more proficient students with greater self-efficacy. Proficiency and self-efficacy comprise the dual goal of differentiation.

> Differentiation, fully understood, is concerned with developing not only content mastery but also student efficacy and ownership of learning... Teachers in effectively differentiated classes help students participate in the formation of their own identity as learners. As students come to trust that process, they develop the power and agency they need to become intellectual beings and thus to own the process of learning. (Tomlinson, 2008, p. 30)

An emotional connectedness is associated with differentiation, a thoughtful approach to teaching. For example, through experience with differentiated instruction, students

- begin to trust that the teacher is on their side

- learn that the teacher knows what motivates them and what they are interested in, and understands what they are ready for

- begin to see the teacher as a partner in the learning process who is continually building personal relevance within a prescribed curriculum

Tips for Communicating with Parents

- Educate parents about the goals of differentiation. Once they understand the guiding principles behind differentiation, they will have little to question.

- Help parents understand the fundamentals of what differentiated instruction is and is not. Their understanding will enlighten them to the ways in which you will personalize the learning experiences of their children. Be clear that different content, a different process, a different product, or a different environment does not mean different learning. The learning is the same, but the way in which their children achieve that learning can vary.

- Rather than simply relying on pre-assessment methods and tools, take the time to talk to parents about the ways their children like to learn and the things their children are saying about school. Sometimes, the conversation around the dinner table can reveal some critical information for a student's success.

- Give parents the opportunity to help their children choose topics, methods, processes, or even specific content that will satisfy the intended learning, as well as their children's personal preferences.

Guiding Questions for Individuals or Learning Teams

1. How do you imagine striking a balance between the need to plan your instruction (scope-and-sequence) with the need to adapt your instruction to the needs of the individual learners (differentiated instruction)?

2. Describe the ways in which you are already differentiating instruction. What positive results have you noticed? What challenges still exist?

3. What makes a task respectful? How can flexible groupings and continual assessments be used to develop respectful tasks?

4. Of the five myths of differentiated instruction identified in this chapter, which was (or is) the most difficult for you to overcome? If differentiation is going to be implemented in your school or district, which myth will demand the most attention?

5. What methods do you currently use (or anticipate using) to learn about student interest, readiness, or learning profile? If you were to do more of one thing, what would it be?

6. How does the phrase "Ignorance on fire is better than knowledge on ice" apply to getting started with differentiated instruction? How do we make sure that our ignorance on fire is not misguided?

Suggested Readings for Further Study

- *Start Where They Are: Differentiating for Success with the Young Adolescent* by Karen Hume

- *The Differentiated School: Making Revolutionary Changes in Teaching and Learning* by Carol Ann Tomlinson, Kay Brimijoin, and Lane Narvaez

- *Leading and Managing a Differentiated Classroom* by Carol Ann Tomlinson and Marcia B. Imbeau

- *Differentiation: From Planning to Practice, Grades 6–12* by Rick Wormeli

Chapter 6

Student Ownership Matters

> *Just as turning over the keys to the family car to a teenager can be both rewarding and risky, turning over ownership of learning to students calls for finesse. We must balance freedom with responsibility if we are to encourage the self-directed learners that the modern world demands.*
>
> **Marge Scherer**

Throughout the entire learning process—from formative assessment to instruction to grading—students need to be equal participants and take ownership over their own learning. After all, it is *their* learning. Traditionally, teachers decided where students sat, what students learned, when students would learn it, how students would learn it, how students would demonstrate what they knew about it, which answers were correct, and which answers were *more* correct. Students were typically passive participants in their own learning, perceived as empty knowledge recipients.

Much of that traditional approach has changed over the past decade. We have collectively learned about the importance of student engagement and connectedness, and the role they both play in student motivation. We have learned that students can be an integral part of their own learning, making it occur in a relevant and interesting way. Student ownership is not about having the students do more of the teacher's work; rather, it is about deepening the role of the student so that the student becomes the creator of meaning within the instructional process. Active learning is about students taking ownership before, during, and after learning has occurred. That way, they understand clearly what they are supposed to know, how to manage it within the process itself, and how to monitor and articulate their progress to date. Like this chapter, which sits rooted in the middle of this book, student ownership needs to be embedded throughout a student's learning continuum.

Big Idea: Meaningful Ownership over Learning

While some teachers are leery of student ownership and are afraid to give up control of the learning for fear that students may choose the easy or least aversive path, the research doesn't support this fear. On the contrary, research suggests that students become more engaged and task focused when they are allowed to make responsible decisions (Guskey & Anderman, 2008). Student ownership has nothing to do with giving up control; it is more about students becoming active partners in the learning process. The teacher ultimately is still responsible for guiding and facilitating the students throughout their learning.

Ownership means creating the conditions that empower students to authentically feel as though their education is something on which they have input and influence. While a teacher's capacity to reach all learners remains an integral part of the teaching and learning process—arguably, the most important factor in student achievement—students can own their learning by taking an active role from start to finish.

Enabling Students to Make Key Learning Decisions

What is worse than not allowing students more involvement in and ownership over their own learning is to involve them in only trivial ways. In student ownership, students are meaningfully involved in every step of the learning process. Ownership moves students beyond the role of participant to a place where they are the primary drivers of their own education—the primary decision makers on important aspects of their learning. As discussed in Chapter 5, some aspects of the curriculum are prescribed and, therefore, students have little input. If, however, there is the option to differentiate the content, let the students decide what they want to learn, and if there is an option to differentiate the process, the products, or the environment, give students ownership over those choices. Our role moves from authority figure who decides *everything* to more of a facilitator who sets the conditions for maximum success. We make sure the required learning occurs and the necessary skills are attained, but students are allowed inside the learning process.

Promoting Student Ownership *Before* Learning

From the outset of this book, I have emphasized student confidence and the role it plays in a student's ability to succeed. Before learning occurs, students must feel confident that they can learn what they need to learn. Part of this confidence comes from a past record of success. The other part of this confidence comes from making clear the intended learning targets—Chapter 3 highlighted the importance of student-friendly learning targets.

Student ownership and involvement can deepen when students write the student-friendly learning targets, either themselves or with assistance from the teacher. The challenge is to understand the learning outcomes in the curriculum guides before converting them. However, the process of making sense of those outcomes will undoubtedly deepen their own clarity. Finding meaningful ways to involve students in the planning of learning helps them feel a sense of empowerment and partnership that recognizes their voice and perspective. The more alternatives we give students for participating in their learning, the more engaged they become (Vokoun & Bigelow, 2008).

Using Self-Assessment for Targeted Ownership

The most critical formative moments occur while learning is taking place. Descriptive feedback and differentiation comprise the focus of the previous two chapters. Both matter significantly when it comes to students maximizing their success. We know that descriptive feedback is most effective when students still have time to act upon that feedback. However, self-assessment goes one step beyond descriptive feedback. When students can self-assess their progress, they will experience true student ownership during the learning process.

For students to know and internalize the expected learning, they must be able to measure their success against the established standards. Heidi Andrade (2007–2008) emphasizes the importance of distinguishing between self-assessment, which is formative, and self-evaluation, which is summative and involves students giving themselves a grade. Without this understanding, some misconceptions emerge:

> Confusion between the two has led to these misconceptions about self-assessment that make many teachers hesitant to try it: (1) Students will just give themselves As, and (2) They won't revise their work anyway, so there is no point in taking the time for self-assessment. (Andrade, 2007–2008, p. 60)

Andrade makes it clear that these misconceptions, unfortunately, can be true if the results of the self-assessment are counted toward a grade or if students are not given the time or help with revisions. If self-assessments *count*, they are no longer formative. Andrade adds that students can actively self-assess and effectively revise if they

- understand the value of self-assessment

- are taught how to self-assess

- share the teacher's understanding of quality

- have the support needed to improve their work

Jan Chappuis (2009) comments on the role of student self-assessment, as well. Chappuis suggests that student self-assessment should always focus on improving features of the work as they relate to the learning targets, not on getting a better score or grade. If students do the learning, the grade will follow.

While teachers may worry that students will give themselves artificially high grades or scores when they self-assess, students must be able to justify their self-assessments. The important point is that self-assessment is formative and therefore doesn't count. If self-assessment doesn't count, then students have no incentive to artificially inflate their assessment results.

As we teach students to self-assess and interact with the learning targets, we also need to teach them how to identify those elements within their work. Once they can justify their assessments, students will have a greater sense of targeted ownership over their learning. Giving themselves a score, checking boxes, or circling numbers is easy; being able to justify their assessment decisions is much more difficult. Therefore, it is important to teach students what is expected and at the same time identify the specific aspects of quality that should be included and must be identified during their self-assessments.

Allowing Students to Communicate Their Progress

Ultimately, student ownership is measured by students' ability to communicate to others about the progress they have made throughout their learning. While they can do this in more formal settings, such as student-led conferences, opportunities to communicate levels of success present themselves almost daily within a less formalized structure or event. By providing students with the opportunity to communicate their learning, we maximize both short- and long-term learning goals:

> Teachers are encouraged to involve students in communicating their learning in different ways because this activity supports student learning in the short term by increasing the feedback they receive, and in the long term by giving them practice presenting themselves as learners. Students are able to talk about and show evidence of their strengths and their learning needs and goals. When students learn, self-assess, and later, when ready, show their learning and receive descriptive feedback, they are developing the skills and habits of self-directed, independent, lifelong learners. (Davies, 2003, p. 2)

Self-directed, independent, lifelong learners are able to

- communicate the intended learning outcomes and criteria for success—criteria that they likely played a role in developing

- describe the progress they have made in relation to the criteria or outcomes

- self-reflect and -assess to set future learning goals and continue to measure their success

Self-reflection leads to a deeper understanding of the concepts taught and a feeling of control of the conditions for learning; it also identifies the *next steps* in the process. The assessment for learning process, taken to scale, allows students to be the primary managers of their own learning. Students can use the assessment information in a variety of ways, such as these:

- setting goals

- making learning decisions related to their own improvement

- developing an understanding of what quality work looks like

- self-assessing

- communicating their status and progress toward established learning goals (Chappuis & Stiggins, 2002)

The person who does most of the assessing does most of the learning. We need to put students in the *ownership and involvement* position to maximize their learning both of the required skills and content, and of themselves.

Putting It into Practice

Teachers can promote student ownership by actively engaging students in setting and understanding assessment criteria.

Most of us can recall a time when we got back a paper that had a score but no feedback or explanation. Nothing indicated how the grade was arrived at, what was good about the paper, and what needed improvement.

Since then, much more knowledge about effective instruction, assessment, grading, and the importance of student ownership and involvement has become available, and with that knowledge comes a responsibility for us to move forward. Students today want choice, options, and opportunities, and they are usually willing to take on appropriate levels of ownership and responsibility.

Too often, the real impediment to increased student involvement and ownership are the adults within the system. The issue, as discussed earlier, is about losing control. I used to think it was my job to control every aspect of instruction from front to back. As I gained experience and learned the real meaning of control, I was able to empower students while maintaining a strong presence within the learning of each student in my class. Teachers and administrators need to catch up to the research findings. They need to validate the student's vital role before, during, and after learning has occurred. Student ownership leads to empowerment, which leads to increased motivation, interest, and commitment.

More Than One Way to Teach

Meaningful ownership comes when you allow students inside the instructional process. Students might, for example, be required to write a persuasive essay, but in most cases, there are options within the assignment that allow students to choose the topic of their essay. By doing so, students are more likely to be motivated to complete the assignment. There are cases, however, where choice of topic may not be an option. In a particular unit, for example, a social studies teacher might want the students to write an essay comparing the advantages and disadvantages of capitalism versus communism. In this case, choice of topic may not be possible, but student ownership and involvement can be enhanced when students become active participants in the instructional process before completing the required assignment.

There are two basic ways to teach students how to write any essay. One way is to deliver information about the structure and content of the assignment. By lecturing and providing checklists and guidelines, a teacher *tells* the students what to do and when to do it. For many teachers, this approach might represent the most efficient means of covering the necessary curriculum. It puts students in the role of *passive recipient*, however—students are told what to do; then, they are expected to apply their acquired knowledge in their own way at some point in the future.

Another, more active way for students to learn is to immerse them in examples of what is expected. For example:

- Provide students with examples of strong and weak comparative essays.

- Provide students with the scoring guide or rubric to be used.

- Ask students to read and assess each paper against the established criteria, so the students interact with all of the necessary elements before producing their own work.

- Once the students have scored the example, reveal how you scored the assignment.

- Engage students in a discussion about what elements they found and which ones they missed.

There are several advantages to this more active process. First, when you provide the scoring guide ahead of time, students see clearly what they are expected to produce, including the specific criteria and how the grades are going to be determined. Even better is the opportunity to co-construct the criteria ahead of time. Second, by being given examples of strong and weak work, students see first-hand what success does and doesn't look like. Finally, students learning in this way are more likely to internalize the criteria of the assignment and be better prepared to produce quality work.

This active approach is just one example of how to create a meaningful lesson that allows active participation in the instructional process. Letting students own the pre-learning process as much as possible sets the stage for them to monitor their own learning and to understand what requires more attention during the learning.

Extending Ownership over Next Steps in Learning

As a math teacher, even after a formal unit test, I would have students go over their test and identify the areas in which they were strong and weak. The end result was that all of my students rewrote the test after some targeted work to address areas of concern or challenge. To identify their strengths and challenges, I had the students complete their self-assessments and develop their learning plans before the re-test. Figure 6.1 (see next page) shows an example of part of a Measurement Unit Plan test review that I gave to my Grade 8 students once they had written the unit test and I had returned it to them. The number of questions on any test, of course, determines the length of the test review.

The routine was quite simple.

1. Students looked at each question on a test and identified whether they got the question right or wrong.

2. If they got the question correct, they moved to the next question. If they got the question wrong, they decided whether it was because they had made a simple mistake or because they needed more study. A simple mistake is when students knew what to do, followed the correct process, but ended up with the wrong answer. Needing more study indicates that students looked at the question and had no idea what to do, or guessed their way through answering the question. Either way, the decision between simple mistake and more study is important, as it determines the level of emphasis each topic would receive.

Figure 6.1: Sample Test Review

Math 8—Measurement

What are my strengths? What are my areas for improvement?

Name: _____   Date: _____

Please look at your corrected test and mark whether each problem is right or wrong. For the problems you got wrong, decide whether it was wrong as a result of a *simple mistake* or whether you need *more study*.

Problem	Learning Target	Right?	Wrong?	Simple Mistake?	More Study?
1	**Perimeter:** I can calculate the perimeter of a triangle.				
2	**Perimeter:** I can calculate the perimeter of a quadrilateral (rectangle).				
3	**Perimeter:** I can calculate the perimeter of a circle.				
4	**Area:** I can calculate the area of a quadrilateral (square).				

Source: Adapted from "You Be George" Activity, *CASL Training* (March 2005), Assessment Training Institute.

Figure 6.1 (continued)

Problem	Learning Target	Right?	Wrong?	Simple Mistake?	More Study?
5	**Area:** I can calculate the area of a quadrilateral (rectangle).				
6	**Area:** I can calculate the area of a quadrilateral (parallelogram).				
7	**Area:** I can calculate the area of a triangle.				
8	**Area:** I can calculate the area of a circle.				
9	**Pythagorean Theory:** I can use the Pythagorean theory to calculate the third side of a right triangle.				
10	**Perimeter and Area:** I can find the perimeter and area of a composite figure.				

My job is to help students determine the difference between them. Many students often struggle with making the distinction, but over time, they become effective at identifying where they went wrong.

3. Once students complete the review, they complete a summary page/learning plan that synthesizes their test results and sets out a plan of action before the re-test (see Figure 6.2). They identify the individual learning targets that they met successfully, which leads them back to the student-friendly learning targets from the beginning of the unit and allows them to see progress.

4. Next, students identify the learning targets they were good at meeting, but need to review since simple mistakes occurred and success was compromised. Once those targets are identified, students need to determine how to stop the same simple mistakes from occurring over and over again—this is where the teacher needs to do some coaching. The eventual goal, of course, is to have the students independently determine the most effective means of avoiding simple mistakes.

   One way is to *teach* students how to review their work. We usually tell our students to check over their work when they are finished, but the bigger question is, how many of us have taught our students how to do that? If they don't know how to review their work, students will likely look it over without any action. With the math example, students should check to see whether their answer makes sense or whether it fits within the equation. Once I teach them *how*, simple mistakes are either corrected or minimized.

5. Students then identify the targets they need to study more: the targets they don't understand and for which they require teacher intervention to learn how to improve their ability to perform the task, make the calculation, or produce the work.

   This is where I spend most of my time. Between the first test and the re-test, I work with small groups of students who have similar challenges on each of the learning targets. Reteaching occurs, but it occurs in a smaller setting at the front or back of the room. This second opportunity is more interactive and intimate; something has to be different to expect an improved result. While I work with the small groups, the remainder of the class works on review, either individually or as small groups. The students who performed extremely well on the original test are given a choice: to challenge themselves with work beyond their grade level or to work as peer tutors and support the students who still struggle.

6. In the end, I ask all of the students to rewrite the test as a way of validating their learning.

As this process played out within my classroom, students learned more about themselves as students than they had at any other time. They began to recognize strategies to avoid simple mistakes; they began to recognize during the initial instruction that they needed more study before the first test. Student responsibility and ownership increased as they became more skilled at recognizing their own learning style, preferences, and challenges.

Figure 6.2: Test Summary/Learning Plan

I am good at...
Learning targets I got right:

I am good at these, but need to do a little review
Learning targets I got wrong because of simple mistakes:
What I can do to keep this from happening again:

I need to keep learning these
Learning targets I got wrong and I'm not sure what to do to correct them:
What I can do to get better at them:

Source: Adapted from "You Be George" Activity, *CASL Training* (March 2005), Assessment Training Institute.

Myron Dueck, a high-school vice-principal who still maintains a partial teaching assignment, points to the reorganization of his summative tests as one of the most significant changes he has made in his career. As Myron describes the changes, it's easy to see how the organization of his tests is more logical and why the students feel a greater sense of ownership after the fact.

For the first decade of his teaching career, Myron constructed tests by section, based on the type or style of the question, which is not dissimilar to how most teachers organize their tests. For example, Myron would have typically organized his unit tests as follows:

Section 1: True & False   (10 pts)
Section 2: Multiple Choice   (15 pts)
Section 3: Short Answers   (10 pts)
Section 4: Long Answer/Essay   (20 pts)

In each of the first three sections, Myron would take a random sampling of concepts and facts from throughout the unit being tested. Therefore, from each section he had a basic idea of what the student knew of the unit as a whole. The last section could be general or specific, depending upon the unit of study. These tests were fairly easy to create and even easier to score.

Myron now organizes his tests by the learning outcomes or standards he wants to evaluate. A test on the United States in the 1920s, for example, is structured as follows:

Section 1: The United States in the 1920s   (11 pts)
Section 2: Causes of the Great Depression   (8 pts)
Section 3: FDR's Efforts to End the Depression   (6 pts)
Section 4: Reactions to FDR's Actions   (7 pts)
Section 5: FDR's Overall Impact on the United States   (11 pts)

Once students receive their test results, the students note their section scores on a custom tracking sheet (see Figure 6.3 on pages 98 to 99, which provides a geography example). They allot each section a percentage score and compare this score to their overall test score, as well as their academic goal. Taking all of these numbers into account, as well as any other factors that may have influenced the outcome (e.g., sports trip, family issues, or academic load), students have significantly more ownership over the next steps as they determine which section(s) to re-test. Students each have the opportunity to plan what they might do differently in preparation for the subsequent evaluation.

Myron believes this reorganization of tests and the routines that follow are important for several reasons. For example:

1. Since students are evaluated according to each learning outcome, teachers can reteach sections (learning outcomes) upon which the entire class scored poorly or below competency, individual students can re-test a single section or multiple sections depending on how they performed, students can easily identify and focus upon the areas in which they know they can improve, and teachers can effectively and efficiently administer re-tests, only re-testing and re-marking those sections that have been identified.

2. Struggling learners usually start with the section they are most proficient at, which increases their confidence and capitalizes on their strengths.

3. Teachers can quickly evaluate if there is a strong correlation between the value of each section and the time allotted to it in class.

4. From the teacher's perspective, re-tests are easy to administer since the teacher constructs them with the same sections and values, but with different questions or question formats.

5. The students feel a much greater sense of ownership and control than is present in conventional testing formats.

■ ■ ■

Figure 6.3

Social Studies 9 Geography Test Tracking Sheet

Name: _____ Date: _____

Topic	Value	Score	%	Re-test?
Grids, latitude, and longitude	20			
Directions	5			
Time zones	10			
Scale	6			
Contours	11			
Climate graph	5			
Canada cities, provinces, water…	7			

Total points _____ out of 64   **Overall test score:** ____ %

Preparation:

Goals and Strategies:
What **overall grade** (percentage or letter) am I hoping to achieve in this course? _____

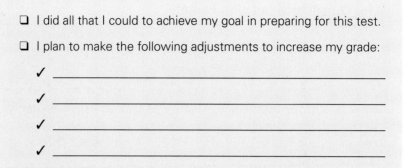

❑ I did all that I could to achieve my goal in preparing for this test.

❑ I plan to make the following adjustments to increase my grade:

✓ _____

✓ _____

✓ _____

✓ _____

The results for Myron have been significant. Students react positively to his new system and embrace the increased ownership they have over their learning. Parents are overwhelmingly supportive of this change, as it obviously gives their children an authentic way to improve their grades. Myron has also seen an increase in the number of students who choose to take part in relearning activities, which demonstrates a desire to learn. Furthermore, students feel reduced anxiety and pressure at the time of the first evaluation.

Differentiating Student Ownership

It is important to ensure that the level of ownership and responsibility expected of students is age appropriate and reasonable, given the individual student's ability and current standing. Student ownership should also be differentiated—some students are not ready to take full ownership of their learning. When students aren't ready, teachers will always be there to support, guide, encourage, and fill in. Assuming ownership and responsibility should be a gradual process over time whereby students gain the necessary confidence to move forward. As we begin to release control, we don't lose our influence. Rather, we begin to ask the right questions instead of giving the answers; we provide opportunities instead of giving specific direction.

Tips for Communicating with Parents

- Communicate to parents which aspects of learning their children are supposed to be responsible for.

- As you begin to phase in an increasing amount of student ownership, allow parents the opportunity to work with their children from home. Keeping parents informed about the changes and enhancements being implemented will go a long way in helping them support their children at home.

Guiding Questions for Individuals or Learning Teams

1. Reflect on your own experience in school. How much of your learning did you have responsibility for? Were there any opportunities for you to contribute to the planning of lessons, the learning process, or the communication of results?

2. In what ways are students *active* decision-makers within your current instructional routines? What new ideas do you have to implement to enhance your students' active involvement?

3. How could student self-assessment be incorporated into your classroom? Describe some of your personal experiences with self-assessment or self-evaluation. Include both positive and challenging experiences.

4. In what ways do students take responsibility for communicating their progress to others? What new ideas do you have to implement to enhance your students' communication of progress?

5. At which point along the instructional continuum—before, during, after—do you find it easiest to provide opportunities for meaningful ownership? Which is the most challenging?

6. What steps will you take to create more opportunities for meaningful student ownership within your instructional routines?

Suggested Readings for Further Study

- *Implementing Student-Led Conferences* by Jane M. Bailey and Thomas Guskey

- *Seven Strategies of Assessment for Learning* by Jan Chappuis

- *Never Work Harder Than Your Students and Other Principles of Great Teaching* by Robyn Renee Jackson

Chapter 7

Accurate Grades Matter

> *It is at minimum essential that all teachers in every school teaching the same grade or same subject/course should determine grades in similar ways and apply similar or the same performance standards.*
>
> **Ken O'Connor**

The intent of this chapter is not to debate the merits of grading. While some might argue that any focus on grades will inherently impede the learning process for students, the intent here is to find, within our existing grading systems, the soundest grading practices to accurately communicate student grades. The assumption in this chapter is that periodic, summative assessments are necessary to verify that learning has occurred and to report to parents (and others) the level of achievement attained by individual students.

Most of us received little, if any, training on sound grading practices and the accurate reporting of student progress. Developing sound grading practices has emerged as a priority since so many other instructional routines and practices, including assessment for learning and differentiated instruction, are redesigning our priorities. In essence, new instructional routines will produce new grading and reporting routines.

While assessment for learning and sound grading practices can work cohesively in a comprehensive instructional system, it is important to remember that they are not the same. As previously discussed, assessment for learning happens during the learning

©P

process. It is designed to inform students and teachers of *where students are* along the learning continuum. The purpose is formative: to inform instruction rather than to report student progress. Sound grading practices, on the other hand, are designed to support the *summative* assessments that occur at the end of the learning. Obviously, with reporting and grade production as their priority, they sit diametrically opposed to assessment for learning in terms of their function within the instructional process.

Sound grading practices, when implemented appropriately, can, however, work seamlessly with formative assessments. At their best, assessment for learning and sound grading practices create the most optimum learning environment and routines to accurately assess and report student achievement.

Big Idea: Accurate and Clear Reporting

Reporting to parents about student progress is one of our most important jobs. Verifying that learning has occurred is a necessary part of the educational process. Most reporting structures require teachers to summarize a term or a semester's worth of learning into one symbol, usually a percentage or a letter grade. Given that, sound grading practices are critical if parents and students are to make accurate interpretations of those symbols. When grades are not deliberately connected to learning, they provide little valuable feedback regarding students' academic strengths and weaknesses (Winger, 2005). Grades need to be meaningful, but they lose their meaning when they are either inflated or deflated for reasons not connected to the intended learning.

Consider two students, both taking the same course with the same teacher. Both earn the same grade, let's say, 78 percent. One might assume that both students achieved the same level of mastery over the content of the course. While their work would not be identical, one might assume that in the end, they both had about the same knowledge of the course content. After all, in most jurisdictions, a grade is supposed to reflect a student's ability to meet the learning outcomes.

Too often, however, two students who earn the same grade arrive at that point from very different directions. Let's use the grade of 78 percent as an example. It is possible that one student earned 88 percent, but for negative reasons not connected to the intended learning, the grade was deflated to 78 percent. It is also possible that the other student earned 68 percent, but for positive reasons not connected to the intended learning, the grade was inflated to 78 percent. So, while their mastery of content is far from similar, the students will both receive the same grade on their report card.

The Need for Grade Interpretation

Furthermore, these positive and negative *non-learning* factors are magnified when used within a strict percentage system. The percentage system creates an overreliance on number crunching and doesn't allow for grade interpretation. Most teachers, without citing the number of incorrect questions or the formulas and weighting used for calculation, could not describe the difference between a student who receives 73 percent and a student who receives 79 percent. With that, it is more likely that our grades lose their meaning and accuracy when reported to others.

In education, we have never been more clinically sound. With our electronic grade books and other advancements in technology, we have up-to-the-second updates and efficiencies never experienced before. Efficiency, however, does not always ensure effectiveness. We have collectively given up much of our decision-making authority to electronic data-collection tools. We are hired, however, not just for our instructional capabilities, but for our professional judgment. Number crunching needs a filter—a compass—that prioritizes which evidence of learning should matter more.

The art of teaching is, among other things, being able to make professional judgments that consider the numbers, but don't solely rely on them. The art of teaching is reporting "pass" when the numbers say "fail." The art of teaching is reporting "not ready" when the numbers say "ready." The art of teaching, from a grading and reporting perspective, means interpreting the numbers and comparing them to what you know to be true.

Putting It into Practice

Teachers should represent students' grades accurately, avoiding practices that inflate or deflate grades.

Remembering that accuracy is the most important aspect to any grade, we need to be mindful of the unintentional ways in which we misrepresent our students' accomplishments. Both grade *inflation* and *deflation* are issues that teachers need to be aware of; both distort achievement results, both present inaccurate grades, and both send mixed messages to students and parents.

My cumulative experience has led me to the point where I no longer use grading practices that either inflate or deflate grades. That, however, wasn't always the case. I have used many of the practices that I am encouraging you to discontinue: group grades, bonus points, attitude points, late penalties, and zeros. The reason I no longer use those practices is that I'm convinced they don't work—the results I wanted never materialized. In fact, the practices proved to be counterproductive, with the response from students usually the opposite of what I had hoped for.

How Grades Are Inflated

Most grade inflation occurs as a result of good intentions. Teachers care about students and want to find as many ways as possible to help them succeed. While the intent is honourable, grade inflation contributes to grades that do not accurately or clearly identify a student's level of performance. The three most common ways that grades are inflated are through group grades, bonus points, and a consideration of student attributes. These issues are discussed below.

1. **Group Grades:** While group grades can inflate or deflate grades, most often they result in students being carried to a high grade. Grades are meant to communicate an individual student's ability to meet the learning outcomes of a particular assignment or course. Group grades don't accomplish this.

Even when working in cooperative groups, students should be graded individually. Individual accountability increases individual participation, helps to equalize participation, and eliminates the problems of the freeloader and the workhorse (Kagan, 1992).

2. **Bonus Points:** Grades must reflect the intended learning and the belief that school is about achieving a high level of learning. Extra credit and bonus points stem from the belief that school is about doing the work and accumulating points, and that quantity is the key (O'Connor, 2007). Bonus points usually serve to boost a student's grade in a way that is either disconnected from or on the periphery of the learning. High grades should be the result of consistently high levels of achievement. If students gain raised grades, the grades should be the result of extra evidence of achievement, not extra points. Clarity is compromised when bonus points are accumulated in ways that have nothing to do with the intended learning, perhaps through attending regularly, helping the teacher after school, asking a lot of questions in class, or answering trivial questions unrelated to the topic at hand. When the desire to further learn is expressed, it is our responsibility to provide the structure so students might redo, relearn, or rewrite. When we do that, we reinforce the view that grades are a communication tool, not the goal (Winger, 2005).

3. **Student Attributes:** Another way in which grades can be inflated is when we choose to include various student attributes as part of the grading and reporting process. Most often, these attributes have more to do with something a student has done—a behaviour—rather than something the student has learned. Class participation and attendance are among the countless examples that exist within our system.

   Our grading dilemma is really twofold: the "nice kid who tries hard" versus the "disruptive student who excels." These two scenarios test the accuracy of our grading systems. On the one hand, we want to help the "nice kid who tries hard" as much as we can, even if it means awarding partial points or including elements unrelated to the learning. While we may be well intentioned, this student's grade will not be accurate and will likely misrepresent the student's ability. On the other hand, disruptive or non-compliant students who achieve high levels of performance can frustrate teachers. We value respect, cooperation, and a positive attitude, so when those qualities are missing, we may begin to think about why a student does or does not *deserve* to receive a high grade.

Students deserve a high grade if they consistently demonstrate high levels of achievement, regardless of other attributes that may serve to buoy a grade. Student attributes are important and should be reported to parents and others; however, they should be reported separately from the grades students earn as a result of their learning.

How Grades Are Deflated

From my experience, grade inflation is not as common as grade deflation. Many of the ways in which grades are deflated are embedded in our traditional practices. Teachers take grading seriously, so to question their accuracy is deeply personal. As such, some teachers feel justified in employing many of the practices as a means of sending the right message or teaching students a life lesson. I'm not suggesting that the message is not right or that the lesson is not important; however, the end result is usually a grade that is inaccurate in relation to the intended learning. Despite the attempts to justify the reasons, grade deflation is more common than most would like to admit.

The practices outlined in the previous section can just as easily deflate grades as inflate them. Group scores for high achievers can pull their overall grades down, while poor behaviour or attitude can reduce the perceived level of achievement. If the *inflation* practices are embedded, then the absence of those attributes could serve a *deflation* role when it comes to grading and reporting.

That said, a few common practices are widely used and contribute greatly to the deflation of student grades. Two of these grading practices—the overemphasis of grades for practice work and the failure to factor student improvement into grading—will be addressed in chapters 8 and 9. The other two examples are outlined below.

Reducing Grades When Work Is Late

Lowering a grade if the student's work is late adds to grade confusion. A late penalty is more reflective of what a student hasn't *done* rather than what the student *knows*. As outlined earlier, a student's grade is meant to reflect that student's ability to meet the learning outcomes for that particular course. Therefore, students should be graded on the quality of their work, rather than on the timing of its submission.

Without question, students need to learn the importance of deadlines; however, whether students meet a deadline is not reflective of the quality of their work. Obviously, the ideal scenario is that a student correctly completes the work on time. Given the other two potential scenarios—the work is done poorly and handed in on time or done correctly and handed in late—most teachers would choose the latter. Yet, late penalties are still widely applied despite lack of empirical support and a number of reasons indicating they are counterproductive.

Most students appreciate deadlines as they provide structure, timing, and guidance to when and where to complete schoolwork. While some students who excel might struggle with individual deadlines, our most vulnerable learners typically have the greatest number of late penalties applied. This situation creates two issues: first, that the late penalty distorts the student's grade; and second, that the penalty has the opposite effect of the teacher's intent. Most teachers who apply late penalties believe that the threat of having their score reduced for lateness provides an incentive for students to hand in work on time. In reality, the fear of failure typically motivates only the students who are already not failing.

What typically happens is that after a few days, students lose their incentive to complete the work. Imagine you are a student who works to the best of your ability and averages (an issue we'll discuss later) 60 percent on most of your assignments. You would go into any future assignments expecting a grade of around 60 percent. If your assignment is three days late, however, and your teacher applies the traditional 10-percent-per-day late penalty, you would already be, in theory, down to 30 percent before handing it in. What if you are four days late? What if this assignment represents an important piece of evidence that will play a significant role in the grade you will receive for the course? At some point, whether you do the assignment or not, you will achieve the same score!

Teachers are often concerned that without late penalties, a flood of assignments will be submitted right before the end of the term. Remember, though, most students like deadlines and will adhere to them not because of the teacher's threat of a late penalty, but for their own organizational comfort. Most students will do what they can to reduce their own anxiety and to hand work in on time. My experience in several schools is that the flood of assignments never plays out that way. Typically, late assignments involve a handful of students who, with a little extra support and encouragement, will complete their work in a timely manner. The bottom line is that handing in work late is a behaviour that should not factor into a student's grade calculation.

While my preference would be to focus on learning and eliminate the penalty, there are some ways to make the issue of a deadline fair for all students.

1. **Provide a window.** Tell students that an assignment is due next week, Monday to Friday. If it is submitted the following week, it will be considered late. The window provides students with the opportunity to manage their time and balance their busy schedules; they can avoid being penalized because their volleyball game happened to be on the night before the report was due.

2. **Provide extra support ahead of time.** Whether we use a late penalty or not, it is important to provide struggling students with support ahead of the deadline. Be proactive, break larger assignments into doable chunks, and even provide intermittent deadlines that ensure the appropriate pacing.

3. **Spend more time in preparation.** To ensure work is completed in a timely manner, spend more time in preparation for all students. Make sure that the students are clear on directions, setup, and explanations. Give them an opportunity to see exemplars from previous years or to interact with the scoring

guide to be used. Do whatever it takes to ensure quality and reduce the likelihood of a deadline being missed.

With all of that, if a teacher insists on a penalty, I suggest applying a one-percent-per-day penalty. Doing this should satisfy the teacher's need to have a late penalty without grossly distorting a student's level of achievement. The few teachers I have suggested this practice to either said that 1 percent is hardly worth the effort so they eliminated their penalty, or that 1 percent isn't tough enough, thereby exposing why they imposed the penalty in the first place. The latter response reflects the belief that compliance should be rewarded and non-compliance should be punished; however, the punishment paradigm does not produce the academic epiphany hoped for.

Assigning Zero for Work That Has Not Been Submitted

The second way in which grades are greatly deflated and distorted is with the use of zero for work that has yet to be assessed. Assigning a zero for work not handed in is like late penalties, a reflection of what a student hasn't *done*, not what the student *knows*. In this context, zeros are arbitrary and mathematically invalid. So why use them?

> Many teachers see zero as their ultimate grading weapon. They use zeros in grading to punish students for not putting forth adequate effort or for failing to demonstrate appropriate responsibility… Some teachers recognize that assigning zeros punishes students academically for behavioural infractions; nevertheless, most believe such punishment is justified and deserved. (Guskey, 2004, p. 50)

Assigning a zero to something that has not been seen compromises the accuracy of the grade and does so to an unknown extent. Such misinformation can lead only to poor quality decisions about students and learning (O'Connor, 2007). Zero, typically a score far removed from a student's cluster of achieved scores, is what statisticians call an "outlier"; it is mathematically invalid since it lies so far from the mathematical cluster. We will explore this point further in Chapter 9 when we examine the issue of averaging.

Using zero is, in essence, assigning a numerical value to work that has not been seen. Zero is a choice, and while there are school policies that require the assigning of zero under certain circumstances, the fact that such a policy exists is still a matter of choice. No research supports the use of zeros or low grades as effective punishments. Instead of promoting greater effort, zeros and the low grades they yield more often cause students to withdraw from learning (Guskey, 2004).

Consider the cluster of scores presented in Figure 7.1 and notice how a zero, coupled with the practice of averaging, distorts Caroline's grade. For the sake of this example, assume that each assignment is of equal weight and therefore of equal importance to the production of Caroline's report card. Assume, too, that Caroline's teacher uses a traditional method of organizing her grade book by task type (e.g, tests, quizzes, assignments) rather than by standards or learning outcomes, something we will discuss later in this chapter.

After the first six assignments, Caroline has a mean average score of 72 percent. If we were to remove the highest score (#1 at 81 percent), Caroline's grade would drop to 70 percent. That means Caroline's highest score has a 2 percent positive impact on her final grade. Add one zero (#7) to her grade book and her grade drops from 72 percent to 62 percent—a 10 percent negative impact. One more added zero drops her grade to 54 percent. Caroline did the first six assignments to the best of her ability, but with two missing assignments, her grade drops 18 percent. While many teachers who use zero will say that the student has every opportunity to complete the missing work, even some without a late penalty, if the work is not completed by the specified end of term, then Caroline would receive 54 percent, likely a grade that would be more detrimental than helpful to her motivation to learn.

Figure 7.1: Caroline's Social Studies Grade Book

	#1	#2	#3	#4	#5	#6	Avg.	#7	Avg.
Caroline	81	77	67	63	74	70	**72%**	0	**62%**

The zeros, as outliers, have a disproportionate impact on Caroline's report card grade.

A more effective response is to assign an incomplete, or an *I*, to the work not handed in. Figure 7.2 shows Caroline's grade book with zero replaced with *I*.

In this scenario, Caroline still has a 72 percent average, but when assignment #7 is not completed, she receives an *I* for that assignment. Even more effective would be to convert her overall grade to an *I* as well. A marathon runner who is injured after running only 36 kilometres doesn't receive a partial time; a student who hasn't demonstrated all of the necessary learning shouldn't receive a distorted grade. Using an *I* instead of zero satisfies three aspects that typically frustrate students and teachers:

1. **Students want to know their grade.** Regardless of how high or how low, students want to know where they stand. When they receive an *I*, students don't know where they stand, which increases their motivation to complete the work.

2. **The *I* increases student accountability.** No portions of the course can be rendered optional. Every piece of learning is essential and nothing can be omitted.

3. **The grade is the most accurate.** Artificially lowering grades, overweighting other assignments, or simply making a *best guess* all fail the accuracy test. Incomplete is the most accurate as it is the most true—the student is not done.

All three of these reasons show that by not using zero, the teacher signifies to students that they remain accountable and must follow through on their responsibilities to their own learning.

Figure 7.2: Caroline's Social Studies Grade Book—Revised

	#1	#2	#3	#4	#5	#6	**Avg.**	#7	**Avg.**
Caroline	81	77	67	63	74	70	**72%**	I	I

While students are not allowed to ignore missing assignments, they should not be left unsupported either. It is imperative that a teacher, or an entire school, have a system or process in place when students are missing work. Critical to the success of any system is that teachers and schools have the opportunity to respond quickly and effectively. The longer an assignment is left incomplete or a learning outcome is left unmet, the less likely the student is to fulfill it in a meaningful way.

The reality is that an *I* is not always possible. In the end, depending upon the grade level, it may be necessary to insert a zero, which may produce a failing grade. My experience has taught me that we defer to the zero far too soon in our grading routines. I have often been asked about when an *F* should be assigned or an *I* converted. My response is always to suggest that this be done at the end of the course. There is no need to use an *F* or a *0* partway through a course. As we've discussed, it rarely produces the desired result. Even if it does, the risks to student confidence outweigh the reward of a completed assignment being handed in.

I recommend that teachers do everything possible to support vulnerable learners *before* assigning an *F* or a *0*. In the end, some students may not pass; however, we need to be sure that their failure is not the result of grade deflation or any other practice we've chosen to use. If a student is unable to demonstrate most of the learning expected throughout a course, then eventually this student might fail. The reality is that teachers, especially in high school, need to submit grades for the purposes of exams, graduation programs, and university transcripts. For these purposes, an *I* is not permitted; however, up until the point where grade submission is necessary, teachers have the flexibility to manage their grades in the most effective manner.

Even after my conversion to a more learning-focused, support-based instructional model, some students still failed my classes. While I wasn't okay with that, I knew that their failure was not the result of anything I did or didn't do. In the end, we are charged with doing *everything we can* to help students succeed. In some cases, our best efforts fall short.

Cheating in Terms of Grade Distortion

Most schools have policies against any form of academic dishonesty, whether it is cheating or plagiarism. There is no intent to minimize the ethical and moral responsibility that students have to represent their own work. The message sent is that cheating cannot be tolerated and is unacceptable by every stretch of the imagination.

The problem is that most school and district policies on cheating are primarily punitive. As a result, they lead to greater grade distortion, which exacerbates the issue discussed throughout this chapter. Schools need effective response plans and creative policies that minimize the need or desire to cheat.

When cheating goes undetected, it leads to grade inflation—students will perform better than if they had completed the work independently. While we can put many controls in place, there is always *some* opportunity for students to misrepresent their work. While some might cheat out of laziness, consider the mindset most students who cheat must have if they feel their only option to pass an assignment or course is to be dishonest. Cheating is as much an act of desperation as it is a willful breach of rules. As we develop confident learners and balanced assessment and grading routines, the desire to cheat will be greatly reduced and the desire for honest representation will replace it.

When cheating is detected, assigning a zero, withdrawing students from class, or expelling them from school is not an appropriate way to deal with the problem. Cheating must be dealt with as a behaviour through the school or district's code of conduct policy, but not in the grade book. Fundamental, once again, is that grades should be a reflection of a student's ability to meet the learning outcomes; they should not be used as an instrument of reward or punishment. The same "zero principles" apply whether missing work or cheating is the issue. The grade is deflated, it in no way represents what a student does or doesn't know, and it removes the student's responsibility to the work.

This issue is difficult for teachers to grapple with. Many teachers take student cheating personally and feel justified in using punishment both in and out of the grade book. However, our policies on cheating are best served when they are not connected to grades and don't allow students to disengage from completing their assignments. Otherwise, accuracy for these students is unattainable.

Converting Rubric Scores to Grades

As we discussed in Chapter 4, rubrics can be an excellent tool to help organize criteria and provide descriptive feedback to students on any given assignment or task. Rubrics can also organize specific learning outcomes, standards, or benchmarks to allow students to see where they are along their learning continuum. The challenge for most comes when we need to convert a rubric score to a letter grade or a percentage. While many schools and school districts are moving to more descriptive, summative reporting, this approach is more typically found with our younger students. In most educational jurisdictions, most students must receive a letter grade or percentage score to represent their learning. This requirement means that at some point, most rubrics will be converted to a grade or a score.

Teachers often make errors when calculating the conversion of rubric scores to percent grades. When I first began using rubrics, I calculated the scores artificially low, which produced deflated grades and misled students (and others) about how well they were doing. If we take a four-by-four rubric as an example (four specific criteria described at four levels of performance), we can see where many make errors. First, the mistake I made over and over was thinking that the lowest level of performance represents a failing grade rather than a minimal passing level. We have to remember that the first level of performance in any rubric is not *0* and should not plummet the student's grade into oblivion. Mathematical calculation errors are likely the most common way in which rubrics are misused.

Look at Figure 7.3 (see next page). Consider the gap between a student who achieves the highest level (4) on all criteria and one who receives the second-highest level (3) on all criteria. Right away you can see that being just one level off in all four categories creates a 25 percent grade gap between Christine and Patty. Being only one level off in two categories creates a 12.5 percent grade gap between Valerie and Christine. The gaps are too large for what one category can represent. In addition, a rubric can create the illusion that all categories are weighted equally when, in fact, they are not. For any essay *sentence structure* is likely not as important as a *thesis statement* or *developing an argument*; however, on a rubric the items might be treated the same.

We need to make sure we don't oversimplify the conversion of the rubric score to a grade. Once we have moved from *tasks* to *learning*, rubric scores are considered as part of the whole, and mathematical precision is less necessary (a topic also addressed in Chapter 9). Various websites and programs can help teachers with the conversion of rubric scores to grades. The formulas, however, are not always made clear to the user, and the grades, while appearing fairer, are still a bit of a mystery. Some teachers use the most common score as the norm, or they eliminate the highest and lowest scores. The bottom line is that the conversion of rubric scores to grades can be awkward and needs more thought than simple mathematics.

Rather than using strict percentages, Arter and McTighe (2001) recommend developing a *logic rule* to convert a rubric score to a grade. One example of a logic rule (page 80, using a 5-point scale) is as follows: *If a student gets no more than 10% of their scores lower than a 4, with at least 40% 5s, then the student's grade should be an "A."* While described as a "rule," a logic rule is actually a fluid method of converting rubric scores—a method that makes sense. Arter and McTighe recommend teachers come up with their own logic rules and that we not take their examples and adopt them wholeheartedly. Grades need to accurately reflect achievement

Figure 7.3: Comparison of Rubric Scores

Student	Rubric Score	Percentage
Christine	All 4s = 16 of 16	100%
Valerie	4, 4, 3, 3 = 12 of 16	87.5%
Patty	All 3s = 12 of 16	75%

levels and not be misleading. Adding up all of the scores and dividing the sum by the number of points available is a surefire way to misrepresent student achievement, despite its simplicity in execution.

Questioning How the Grade Book Is Organized

Many teachers are moving away from a traditional organization of their grade book. Rather than organizing their grade books by task type (e.g., tests, quizzes, and assignments) and weighting each accordingly, more teachers are beginning to organize their grade books around learning outcomes.

As we shift from tasks to learning, everything, including our grade book organization, has to at least be questioned in terms of how applicable it is within the new paradigm. That does not mean you have to reorganize your grade book to embrace the new learning paradigm; it does mean you have to ensure that logic and thought are behind how achievement is reflected and reported. Many teachers realize, however, that it is more relevant to report on specific learning outcomes, or at least organize around the big ideas of learning.

Across North America, schools and districts are beginning to move to a performance-based reporting process for all of their students. In the name of accuracy, these performance-based reporting processes create greater meaning when it comes to communicating student achievement. By organizing around learning outcomes or standards, we have the ability to collect and track several pieces of evidence that reflect each student's achievement within the specific outcome. Then, when it comes time to report, we can consider all of the evidence with the intent to summarize student achievement most accurately, with the most recent evidence taking priority (a topic explored further in Chapter 9).

How we organize the evidence of learning makes as much of a difference with accuracy as does the evidence itself. As stated above, reorganizing our grade book is not necessary (and with some electronic grade books not even possible), but rethinking how the evidence is communicated will provide a more accurate picture of what each student is capable of.

Tips for Communicating with Parents

- Help parents understand the new ways of reporting and how to interpret the performance-based standards rather than a single symbol. If traditional weighted grade books are in use, some parents, especially if their child's grade is lower than expected, may have difficulty making sense of how the grade was arrived at. They might assume it's the same *total points* approach to grading that they themselves experienced in school.

- Accurately report to parents the progress their children are making; inform them of where their children are along their learning continuum. It should be easy for parents to understand how much progress their children are making.

Guiding Questions for Individuals or Learning Teams

1. In your own experience as a student, have you ever had your grade *deflated* through an aspect unrelated to any of the intended learning outcomes? Describe how you felt and what impact the experience had on your motivation to learn.

2. Of the grading practices you currently use, which has the greatest potential to *inflate* student achievement and inaccurately reflect their learning? What could you do to prevent this inflation from occurring?

3. Of the grading practices you currently use, which has the greatest potential to *deflate* student achievement and inaccurately reflect their learning? What could you do to prevent this deflation from occurring?

4. Discuss the pros and cons of *0* versus *I* in light of your own experience or the issues you anticipate that each might create.

5. How do you currently convert a rubric score to a grade? What is your experience with *logic rules*? If your experience is limited, what method do you think you might use to make this conversion?

6. What is your experience with reorganizing your grade book around learning outcomes as opposed to task types? What were the benefits in terms of accurate reporting? What methods did you use to summarize multiple pieces of evidence of the same learning outcome?

7. How do you (or your school) deal with cheating? Have you explored appropriate responses that avoid the grade book?

8. What are your next steps in terms of accurate grading?

Suggested Readings for Further Study

- *A Repair Kit for Grading: 15 Fixes for Broken Grades* by Ken O'Connor

- *How to Grade for Learning: Linking Grades to Standards, K–12,* 3rd edition, edited by Ken O'Connor

- *Elements of Grading: A Guide to Effective Practice* by Douglas Reeves

Chapter 8

Practice Matters

> *At its best, homework in reasonable amounts can support and enhance learning, provide feedback to teachers about learning, allow students to practice skills and deepen their knowledge, and instill confidence within students when they successfully complete tasks on their own.*
>
> **Cathy Vatterott**

This chapter explores the lost art of *practice* within any classroom environment. Many of us have fallen for the myth that everything a student does must count toward a final grade. *Practice* matters because students need the opportunity to practise new learning without fear of penalty. Allowing for practice gives students the necessary time to interact with new content or skills before being measured on how much they have learned. If practice is paired with descriptive feedback, students will experience an increase in confidence and the deeper understanding necessary for those summative moments when learning is verified.

This chapter assumes that students are going to be assigned homework and practice. Some in education debate the merits of students being assigned any work to be completed at home. While some practice and homework assigned to students is unnecessary and represents busywork more than essential learning activities, most would agree that strategic practice and homework completed at home will benefit students immensely. This chapter focuses on how to more effectively manage the practice paradigm, both in and out of the grade book; it does not intentionally present a view on whether homework and practice *should* be a part of a student's learning experience.

Big Idea: Practice Without Penalty

Practice makes perfect. Whether throwing a baseball, riding a bicycle without training wheels, or jumping rope, most of us were taught that if we practised long enough, in the correct manner, we would eventually master whatever we were trying to learn. The idea was simple: with proper instruction and enough time to practise, everyone will eventually learn. As we got older, of course, we realized that being perfect was not always possible. However, the idea of striving for perfection (or mastery) through appropriate practice is a concept we are unlikely to forget.

Yet, within our traditional routines in school, practice most certainly won't make perfect if the results of practice are overemphasized in the grade book. The only way practice could make perfect in school is if the first attempt is perfect and all subsequent practices are perfect as well. Since most traditional grading routines include the use of averaging (an issue discussed later in this chapter), *imperfect practice* makes it impossible for students' grades to reflect the perfection they may or may not eventually achieve. Being perfect may not be a realistic goal for many of our students, but in a sense, the term refers to students doing the best they can to achieve to the highest level possible. Therefore, if they achieve that highest level, it should be reflected more accurately in the grade book.

Practice Versus Homework

Before going any further, it is important to clarify the difference between *practice* and *homework*. Often these two terms are used interchangeably; however, for the purpose of this chapter, a clear separation of the two is necessary:

- *Practice* refers to those times where students make a first attempt and use or work with new learning. For most of us, this represents some of the traditional homework we used to do and, in some cases, still assign. For example, after teaching students how to add and subtract fractions, the teacher assigns a set of questions from the textbook so students can practise adding and subtracting fractions. Typically, practice assignments lead to the curriculum's big ideas and represent more of a means to an end.

- *Homework* refers to work completed at home that is either an extension or a deepening of the key learning outcomes, or work completed in preparation for a summative assessment. For example, students doing a project on the causes of World War I would likely not have sufficient time to finish in the classroom; therefore, they would complete the project at home.

With this new paradigm come new routines that make the use of practice more efficient and effective. Students who don't learn fast enough are often penalized in the grade book since their first attempt at a new skill is usually far from perfect. As a result, they may undergo a loss of confidence and feel despair since the results show that they didn't achieve a high score. Once we shift our focus, the students will shift as well. Instead of noting a student's first attempt to practise new learning in the grade book, the teacher should provide descriptive feedback on the student's work. Providing students with descriptive feedback is critical to their growth and understanding. With that feedback, provided *during* the learning, practice can make perfect and student grades will be more accurate.

The Limitations of Traditional Homework

The traditional routine around homework didn't typically make the distinction between *practice* and *homework* because everything counted. It also stressed compliance as much as it did learning. The need for homework was not only to provide practice, but to serve as a way to teach students responsibility. While typically not a learning outcome in most curriculum guides, responsibility was viewed as a moral outcome and one that was difficult to argue against. Fundamental to the task-completion paradigm is the notion of completing all tasks that have been assigned. That said, when assigning homework, teachers are making a few assumptions about their students.

> Inherent in the old paradigm are the assumptions that all students can do the work (not all of them can), that all students have the time to do the work (not all of them do), and that students should take as much time as is necessary to do the work (not all of them will). (Vatterott, 2009, p. 91)

These assumptions can make the results of homework, at best, misleading. At worst, if the results are in the grade book and factor into producing a final grade, they can be frustrating for students and subsequently deflate their grades and their desire to learn.

Most teachers are not intentionally deflating grades. The reason most teachers count practice and homework is they feel it will help a student's grade. The idea is that the scores will buoy a student's grade so there is less pressure when it comes to major assignments or summative exams that contribute much to the final grade calculation. In most cases, that belief is true. What is rarely considered, however, is that counting everything the student does could have the opposite effect. If a student is not clear on directions, doesn't understand the concept being taught, or doesn't have the time to complete it, the inclusion of practice in final grade calculations can make things worse.

If completion is overemphasized, students will be more focused on *getting it done* (as opposed to learning), and any grades assigned will distort their achievement. In other cases, as discussed in Chapter 7, the use of zeros or late penalties related to practice or homework can lead to grade deflation and distortion. Since homework in some classes is scored and counted daily, the cumulative effect can be devastating.

Rather than assigning homework from a task completion perspective, the relatively new focus of *practice without penalty* creates a natural extension of the lessons being taught. By our emphasis on the importance of practice, students understand that they can take some chances during the learning process without worrying about the impact on the grade book. By learning from their mistakes, students will be more prepared for their summative assessments, and their grades will be more reflective of what they have learned.

Putting It into Practice

Teachers should be sure to provide descriptive feedback before grading any of students' attempts at practising new learning.

Implementing the *practice paradigm* led me to adopt this idea as a fundamental belief. As both a classroom teacher and school administrator, I had to focus on some fundamental questions and dispel some myths about why practice was important and why emphasizing the grading of practice was misguided.

Exposing the Flaws of Grading Everything

As I began to implement practice as a routine in my own classroom, the flaws of the *grade everything* paradigm were exposed. While some teachers predict that if work isn't graded, then the students won't do it, that wasn't my experience. On the contrary, more students began completing their work as the stress of completion was removed and replaced with a more appropriate focus on learning. Rather than being met with a penalty for incomplete work, students were met with more support to move their learning forward.

Before my decision to implement practice in my classroom, I asked myself some fundamental questions that brought the issue of practice to the forefront.

Whose work was I grading?
When everything counts, the incentive to cheat or deceive is high, especially for struggling students whose primary goal can be to

accumulate enough points to offset any future disasters. In this case, the goal of learning becomes secondary to the goal of finishing. When at home, students have access to parents, siblings, friends, the Internet, and other sources to find answers to the questions they are working on. While many students complete their work, little independent learning occurs, rendering the assignment pointless.

I began to see students whose anxiety around the potential loss of points overruled any desire to learn. Once I took away the grade or points, the incentive to cheat was diminished. Students in my classes quickly realized that cheating had no point if learning and practice were the goal, and the grade from the practice did not factor into a final grade. While some students still copied other students' work, it was much easier to convince those students that cheating was pointless. They came to realize that if there were no points to accumulate, they might was well learn as much as they could, figure out where they were through practice, and receive specific feedback on how to improve. Once the desire for a score is removed, the motivation to learn and practise increases.

Was my instruction really that flawless?

When everything, including practice, counted, what I was really saying was that my instruction was flawless and that I needed to teach a new concept only once to have 30 diverse learners master the content simultaneously. One lesson on any topic without some descriptive feedback will not lead to content mastery by all students in the class. Even a master teacher isn't good enough to think that every skill, idea, or section of content requires only a single lesson to take an accurate measure of how much students have learned. I believe I am a good teacher, but I'm not that good. I've learned that I need to give students the chance to process their initial learning and receive some descriptive feedback from me before I judge whether they have mastered the intended learning outcomes of the lesson.

Were my students clear on directions?

Many times, students have an adequate understanding of a lesson before their first attempt at practice; however, they are not clear on what they are supposed to do. I had to improve in this area, especially with my struggling learners. When assigning practice, I began to see how crucial it was that students were clear on directions. When some of my students were not clear on directions, two results became common: (1) They simply didn't do the work, which meant they didn't practise or enhance their learning and so became further behind; or (2) They completed the practice, but it was incorrect. With this latter result, I started to see bad habits form, which made it more difficult for the students to get back on track. Too often, the assigning of work happens at the very end of a lesson—even sometimes after the bell has rung—leaving little time to explain how to complete the work correctly. When I realized that being clear on directions is important, I took the time to ensure that those students who struggle with directions were clear before they left my classroom.

Should students learn with or without their teacher?

The lack of clarity and directions led some of my students to find other sources to relearn the lesson taught earlier in the day. Clearly, students benefit most if they do most of their learning in their teacher's presence. Only when a teacher is sure that the lesson has been learned and the students are clear on directions should students be left on their own to *show what they know*.

In this area I had to be more strategic about the types of assignments I was sending home and whether or not students were ready to work independently. We know feedback matters—especially timely feedback, which makes it more vital that students do most of their learning in our presence. Students should and can practise at home, but they should not be learning a new skill or section of content on their own. Once I knew they "got it," I felt more comfortable about assigning independent practice.

Work completed at home for summative purposes is a different matter. This work is intended to measure learning and should not have any influence from the teacher. Again, it needs to be an accurate portrayal of what the student knows. Before those summative moments, however, teachers need to remain actively involved through descriptive feedback on practice assignments designed to advance student learning.

Where were my non-graded moments?

While I often encouraged students to be risk takers, to stretch their thinking, my students were more likely to play it safe if everything counted. I became aware that asking students to take an academic risk when it might cost them in the grade book was unrealistic. If everything counts, students, especially struggling learners, are more likely to stay within themselves and not risk a disaster. With the practice paradigm, academic risks become more common because students know that taking them will not affect their grade.

Once my students were given feedback on their new learning, I might count any subsequent assignments on the same content. The assignments had to be directly connected to the intended learning outcomes and have a summative purpose. Otherwise, the emphasis was on practice and creating the non-graded moment, allowing students to relax and try without penalty.

Practice: Implementing a New Routine

Two big myths often enter the discussion about practice: (1) that students don't have to complete any work at home and (2) that students won't do the work if it doesn't count. In fact, students are held more accountable for the learning because the results of their practice are more authentic and their responses are more relevant. As my implementation of the practice paradigm evolved, I settled into a routine in which most students completed their practice and took ownership of their learning. This practice routine brought clarity of purpose to many of the practice assignments I was asking students to complete.

1. **Assign practice with purpose.** While much practice is completed in class, link any practice that has to be completed at home directly to the learning outcomes for that day. In other words, be purposeful about why the students need to complete the practice at home; the students themselves also need to recognize the connection. I found that assigning relevant tasks for practice became important to advance my students' abilities to understand and perform the necessary learning.

2. **Always check practice for completion and correctness.** Take the opportunity to check that the practice has been completed and review it in class. By doing so, I was able to see whose first attempts were successful and who needed more support, more instruction, and more practice. I was also able to provide feedback to ensure greater success next time and even use the practice as a formative tool to determine my next steps in instruction. In some of my classes where the practice assignments focused on a specific skill (e.g., adding and subtracting fractions), I got to a point where students chose whether they would complete all of the practice assignments or not. As they became more proficient and accurate at self-assessment, they determined when no further practice was necessary. Teaching students to self-assess and take ownership, as discussed in Chapter 6, empowers students to monitor their progress.

3. **Record and track the results of the practice.** When students are allowed to monitor their own learning, there is always the risk that their self-assessments are inaccurate. As a result, always record and track the practice results. This information becomes most relevant at those summative moments throughout a unit or teaching cycle. Periodically, I would assign a quiz or an assignment that was intentionally summative, designed to verify that learning had occurred. By tracking and recording practice, I was able to compare the summative assessment results with the practice results. When I had a student who had not completed all of the practice assignments but scored high on the summative assessment, I knew that the self-assessments were accurate and that the practice was unnecessary. On the other hand, I had students whose summative performance was low despite their perception that they understood the material and deemed the practice to be unnecessary. It was obvious to me that their self-assessments were inaccurate and that I needed to spend some time correcting their understanding. The discrepancy in results allowed me to have an authentic conversation with a student about the need to complete the practice assignments: I had information showing the student that the completion of practice assignments was critical to learning and not

simply an issue of compliance. This is yet another way to differentiate and personalize learning.

4. ***Never* count the results of the practice in the grade book toward a final grade.** As discussed, the major shift in my classroom was that practice didn't count. While I favour a grade book organized around learning outcomes and most recent evidence, teachers using a more traditional grade book organized by task type can still implement a practice paradigm within their classrooms. Most electronic grade books will allow different tasks to carry "zero weight," allowing them to be present without factoring into final grade calculations. This way, both formative and summative assignments can be compared to ensure accurate self-assessments by students and to enable teachers to determine next steps in instruction.

Dealing with Practice That Counts

As a high-school administrator, I have seen first-hand the stress and anxiety that surrounds the final exam experience and the role that *practice that counts* plays in distorting achievement. Now more than ever, the classroom and the final exam are two completely different experiences for students. The exam is a one-shot deal, whereas the classroom, by and large, is becoming a place of growth, multiple opportunities, and differentiated learning. As such, I have seen many variations in how students perform in the classroom and how they perform on a final exam. The difference is even more significant in skill-based courses such as math and English, where learning the skill, rather than learning content as in social studies and science, is usually transferable to any variation of the questions.

The variation that intrigued me the most was when a student performed well on a provincial exam yet had an extremely low classroom grade. One example was a student in my school who entered the provincial exam with a low classroom grade (47 percent) but scored 78 percent on the provincial exam. How does that happen? Clearly, the classroom grade didn't reflect the student's ability to meet the learning outcomes of the course. While I'm not espousing the virtues of final exams, skill-based ones can offer a fair reflection of a student's ability, provided the setting, questioning style, and other "exam" factors are controlled for. That said, when a gap such as the one presented in the example appears, it presents a great opportunity to dig deeper.

In the case of the student mentioned above, discussions with the teacher established that the classroom grade was deflated through a combination of late penalties and zeros assigned to missing homework assignments. Since homework in this student's class was scored and counted daily, the cumulative effect was devastating. The 78 percent that the student scored on the provincial exam was an accurate reflection of the student's performance on other summative tests. The classroom grade was low as a result of incomplete practice.

Practice needs to be practice, especially when it comes to new learning—it should not play a role in final grade calculations.

> **B**en Arcuri, a high-school chemistry teacher with whom I have worked for several years, takes a unique approach to practice. Ben's continued shift away from what many would consider "traditional practices" has brought about improved achievement results for his students: results significant enough that he would find it unthinkable to return to how he used to do things. For example, in 2008–09, 95 percent of the students from Ben's classes who wrote the Chemistry 12 exam achieved a passing score—3 percent higher than the provincial average for British Columbia. Further, the students in Ben's classes are developing the confidence to write the exam. In British Columbia, the Chemistry 12 exam is considered optional, so students are not required to write the exam upon completing the course. As Ben has introduced many changes within his classroom, more students are choosing to write the exam. Ben's high school is one of three in School District No. 67. In 2008–09, 80 percent of the students in that school district who wrote the exam were from Ben's classes. Results matter, and the results for the students in Ben's classes indicate that the shift to practice has been a major influence in this upward trend.
>
> The biggest shift for Ben was the introduction of a system of re-quizzing. After teaching a few introductory lessons on a topic in

Chemistry, Ben has the students write a quiz on that topic. When the students return to class the next day, they go through their quizzes to see which aspects of the topic they have mastered and which ones they need further study on. Ben then assigns the students further practice activities based upon each student's needs. A day or two later (or more depending on the breadth and depth of the topic at hand), Ben offers students a re-quiz to check whether or not their further practice has produced a greater understanding. Although this re-quiz is optional, most take it.

Ben's entire teaching load is senior Chemistry (Grades 11 and 12). Ben knows that the composition of his classes is more homogeneous than the groupings found in the younger grades in most high schools. Most of his students are motivated by grades, want to achieve at a high level, and will likely attend a college or university upon graduation. The practice Ben uses is specific to his senior chemistry courses, and he would not implement it the same way if he were teaching a Grade 9 science class.

Ben notes that if he were teaching younger students, he would use the same system but likely implement it in a slightly different way. His comment emphasizes the point that systems are universal, but that practices need to be age appropriate. For his senior students, the quizzes count in the grade book; however, Ben estimates that each quiz is worth only about 0.2 percent toward a student's grade since he gives more than 20 quizzes in a semester. When students write the re-quiz, only the higher of the two scores counts. This approach allows the first quiz, in theory, to be a practice activity. It is assumed that most students' scores will significantly improve on the re-quiz.

Any homework that Ben assigns in his classes is optional. Ben emphasizes to his students that they should do the homework if they believe they have not mastered the learning at hand, as evidenced by their quiz scores. Some students do all of the homework, others only work on what they need to, while others do very little. What Ben emphasizes is self-assessment and self-management. The students know that Ben is always available for more intensive support. However, the age appropriateness of

Ben's system puts the students at the centre of the decision-making process because he believes they are mature enough to take that on.

For students who experience repeated failures or whose re-quiz results show no improvement, Ben takes more of a hands-on approach to determine where things are going wrong. Doing this could involve the parents to make sure that they understand what is necessary to keep their child on track. If a large number of students show poor results, then Ben will go back and reteach the lessons in a way that makes more sense to the students. He recognizes that adjustments to the lessons will be necessary.

While Ben's approach might not be a traditional approach to practice, the results for the students in his classes are compelling. Practice serves as a great opportunity for students to take some risks by stretching their thinking without it costing them on their report card. If everything counts, there is no margin for error, leaving no room to grow. While Ben's quizzes do count, the impact on the students' grades is so minimal that students are more focused on their potential for improvement. Most students would rather play it safe than risk their opportunity to pass; Ben has found a system that creates an environment where risk taking and personal ownership are maximized. Practice can make perfect—or at least a lot better—if we create the right routine and atmosphere that will encourage students to go beyond their own potential.

Tips for Communicating with Parents

- Clearly communicate information to parents to help them distinguish between practice and homework using your website, course outline, or open house when parents come to meet their children's teachers.

- If you use a lot of handouts or blackline masters for practice, copy them on different-coloured paper to help parents know right away that the handouts don't count. Furthermore, if students self-regulate their work by determining when practice is no longer necessary, then

©P

the coloured paper lets parents know that it is okay for their child to stop at question 9 when 14 remain.

- Identify practice activities on your website or blog, or in an email to parents.

- Distinguish between which assignments are essential (that is, will count in the grade book) and which assignments are for practice.

Guiding Questions for Individuals or Learning Teams

1. What routines have you established around practice?

2. What new routines do you think you might add?

3. What is the most positive outcome in allowing authentic practice as part of a student's learning experience?

4. What potential challenges might you anticipate while implementing a *practice paradigm* within your classroom?

5. Why do think some teachers or schools still use a more traditional model where *everything* counts?

6. What next steps are necessary for your school or district to adopt a *practice* mindset and take it to scale?

Suggested Readings for Further Study

- *The Art and Science of Teaching: A Comprehensive Framework for Effective Instruction* by Robert J. Marzano

- *A Repair Kit for Grading: 15 Fixes for Broken Grades* by Ken O'Connor

- *Rethinking Homework: Best Practices That Support Diverse Needs* by Cathy Vatterott

Chapter 9

Improvement Matters

> *If at any time in the instructional process students demonstrate that they've learned the concepts well and mastered the intended learning goals, doesn't that make all previous information on their learning of those concepts inaccurate and invalid?*
>
> **Thomas R. Guskey**

Improvement is fundamental to the teaching and learning experience. All teaching and learning begins with a lack of knowledge and is followed by some form of instruction, which leads to greater understanding or ability, which then signals an improvement in the individual's knowledge or skill. Our traditional systems of grading and reporting provide only limited opportunities for students' improvement to be truly reflected on their report cards. Teachers are now experiencing these limitations and are beginning to implement means that take into account the most recent evidence that truly reflects student growth throughout their learning.

Once again it comes down to the paradigm shift from *tasks* to *learning*. If learning is the focus, then it makes sense that improvement matters and that it be reported to students and parents in a more accurate way. In some cases, students with low grades improve more than students with high grades; however, this pattern is rarely reflected in our reporting process.

It is necessary to clarify that this chapter is not about *improvement scoring* where we calculate an improvement score and use that to determine the grade. This chapter focuses on improvement from the most *recent evidence* perspective and does so without suggesting that improvement be the single factor in determining grades. In essence, it is really about adding another layer of thought to the role that improvement can play within our grading and reporting systems.

Big Idea: Recognizing Improvement in Grading

We know that learning is an individual process that often deviates from our scope-and-sequences of instructional planning. Grades are broken when learning is developmental (likely to improve over time with practice and repeated opportunities) and the final grade does not recognize the student's final level of proficiency (O'Connor, 2007). Our traditional way of teaching, grading, and reporting emphasizes not only what students learn, but when they learn it. Students are penalized if they don't learn fast enough—if they don't keep up with our scope-and-sequence.

While there are curricular pressures to cover the course content, what really matters is that students *learn* something. Most teachers are expert enough in their curricular areas to cover the course material in less time than is allotted to them in a semester or year. Coverage, as we know, is not the primary goal. If the course material is covered, but students don't learn anything, then the coverage (instruction) was pointless. Coverage is the means; learning is the end.

By providing students with the opportunity to demonstrate their improvement, our grading and reporting become more accurate reflections of how students have grown throughout the course. Practice and improvement work hand in hand. By not using practice scores to calculate student grades, we are better able to factor improvement into the grading process.

In many cases, the limited attention paid to improvement is self-imposed. Even teachers who do not factor improvement into their daily routines are usually aware of how improvement *can* factor into their grading practices. Others may believe it is not permitted. Whatever the case, my experience has taught me that the issue around factoring improvement into grades is an issue of awareness. Our system of grade calculation is a significant limiting factor for why improvement isn't part of our grading and reporting. In particular, the practice of averaging (finding the mean score) for final grade calculations suppresses student improvement and, like an anchor, reminds students of what they used to not know.

How Averaging Distorts Achievement

As a result of using the mean average, every score of 40 needs a score of 80 to earn a final score of 60. In other words, students have to outperform themselves by what they often perceive as an unattainable level to earn a grade that they might even be marginally satisfied with. Students who consistently score at a certain level are not likely to feel encouraged and confident about the prospect of doubling their score on the next attempt. Even if the scores are not as extreme, students still see this as a daunting task.

Teachers can use three methods to calculate the average, or central, tendency:

1. The *mean*, or what is often referenced by the term *average*, treats all data the same and is found by adding up the values and dividing by the number of data sets.

2. The *median*, another way to calculate an average, determines the middle score.

3. The *mode* determines the most frequent score.

Figure 9.1 shows an example of a student's grades and how each of these measures of central tendency had an impact on the student's final grade.

Figure 9.1 presents an unusual distribution of scores, but it highlights the inherent flaw in how we traditionally calculate grades. While these calculations will help us determine our students' levels of performance, we should not rely solely on any form of mathematical calculation to determine a student's grade.

Figure 9.1: A Student's Score Three Ways

1	2	3	4	5	6	7	8	9
9%	17%	26%	55%	61%	80%	84%	84%	84%

Mean Score = 50.5%   Median Score = 61%   Mode Score = 84%

Finding the mean is the method most often used for averaging. Clearly, this student is now consistently performing at an 84 percent level; however, the unusually low scores at the beginning of the learning still constitute a huge factor on the score. This points to the challenge with using the mean: the extreme scores have a significant impact on a mean score, and one extremely low score significantly skews the results.

The advantage of using the *median* is that it is not influenced by outliers at the extreme end of the data set. One zero does not alter the student's median score, but does have a sizable impact on the mean score. Figure 9.1 illustrates this fact; the mean score is 10.5 percent lower than the median score.

The disadvantage of using the median score is that it makes no reference to the student's current status. The 61 percent occurred at a point no longer reflective of the student's ability to meet the learning outcomes. The most recent evidence indicates a much higher level of performance.

The advantage to using the *mode* is that it reflects the most common occurrence. In the case of Figure 9.1, the student would benefit from the fact that the mode score represents the most recent evidence of learning—the student would have an 84 percent for the report card. However, what if the student took longer to master the content of the course, which produced a mode score of 26 percent? In that case, the student's exponential growth would be marginalized in favour of the score that appeared most frequently.

The biggest idea here is that all three methods of calculating central tendency have serious limitations. These limitations are magnified if only one method is used almost exclusively, as mean scores are in our school systems. We need to return to a more thoughtful process of calculating grades: a process that allows teachers to consider all three central tendency calculations and use their professional judgment to determine which score best reflects the student's ability to meet the learning outcomes for the unit or subject. This professional judgment has been hampered greatly by the increased use of electronic grade books.

> For all their advantages, however, computerized grading programs also have their shortcomings. Perhaps the most serious is that they lead the educators who use them to believe that mathematical precision necessarily brings greater objectivity and enhanced fairness to grading. Many teachers assume that, so long as the mathematical calculations are correct and all students are treated the same, then the grades assigned are accurate and just. But numerical precision is not the same as evaluative fairness, honesty, or truth. (Guskey, 2002, p. 776)

Giving the student referred to in Figure 9.1 a grade of 50.5 percent would be mathematically precise; however, it falls short of providing a fair grade that truly reflects what the student has accomplished.

Start with the Highest Score, End with the Highest Grade?

Another ripple effect of using the mean score as the exclusive method of averaging is that students who earn high scores early in the learning have an advantage. Consider the scenario presented in Figure 9.2, which shows how three students performed on eight units of study and a comprehensive final exam, and what their

Figure 9.2: Mean Scores for Three Students

	Unit 1	Unit 2	Unit 3	Unit 4	Unit 5
Sarah	90%	90%	90%	90%	90%
Heather	50%	55%	60%	65%	70%
Kevin	35%	35%	35%	50%	60%

final mean score percentage would be. No extra weighting has been added to the final exam; it simply factors in equally, as do all of the other unit scores.

Although Figure 9.2 is just an example, you can see that all three students performed at exactly the same level on the comprehensive final exam; they are all leaving the course with a similar ability to demonstrate the learning outcomes for the course. However, when the mean score is used, these students do not receive the same grade.

Performances at the beginning of the course play a significant role in the students' final grades. Heather steadily improved, while Kevin had an incredible turnaround at some point in the middle of the year. The question is, are their grades an accurate reflection of their ability to meet the learning outcomes for the course? It is possible that Sarah, Heather, and Kevin applied themselves to their studies at significantly different levels from the outset, and that is reflected in the discrepancy. It is also possible that each entered the course with various degrees of subject knowledge before any instruction began. Without knowing this, a teacher could inadvertently penalize students for not knowing the course material soon enough. In either case, relying solely on mathematical precision for grade calculation falls short of providing an accurate picture of each student's true ability.

All three students should be graded on their ability to meet the required learning outcomes or standards for each course. It is therefore troubling when recent evidence indicates a high level of performance against the criteria, but previous demonstrations continue to play a significant role in grade determination. This chapter

Figure 9.2 (continued)

Unit 6	Unit 7	Unit 8	Final Exam	Final Grade
90%	90%	90%	90%	**90%**
75%	80%	85%	90%	**70%**
70%	90%	90%	90%	**62%**

(and really, the entire book) is about taking the automaticity out of what we do and replacing it with a more thoughtful examination of how we assess, instruct, and report our students' current abilities to meet the set criteria or intended learning for the classes we teach.

Putting It into Practice

Teachers should exercise professional judgment in determining how to grade student performance.

To control for the limitations of mathematical calculations, some teachers now give significant consideration to the most recent evidence of learning. By doing so, we move beyond simple grade *calculation* and toward what Ken O'Connor refers to as grade *determination*.

> Given the limitations of measures of central tendency to deal effectively with all score distributions and the many factors affecting student performance I conclude that we have to see grading not as simply a numerical, mechanical exercise, but as primarily an exercise in professional judgment. It calls for teachers to demonstrate two key aspects of professional behavior—the application of craft knowledge of sound assessment practice and the willingness and ability to make and be ready to defend one's professional judgment. (O'Connor, 2007, p. 83)

Grade determination is about professional judgment. While number crunching will likely always occur, our professional judgment should ultimately determine the grade.

As a profession, we are steadily improving in the two areas that Ken O'Connor mentions in the above excerpt—knowledge of sound assessment practice and the ability to defend our professional judgment—yet it remains challenging for individual teachers to move beyond their spreadsheets. Although many teachers know and understand more about grading that ever before, there is plenty of evidence of traditional practices and grade calculations (e.g., grading on the curve by not giving out too many *A*s). The willingness to make and defend our professional judgment is a greater challenge. Some teachers aren't prepared to move beyond the calculations for fear of losing the objectivity of the grades. For some, it is important to remain objective and impartial when calculating grades. However, the examples provided in this chapter show there is no such thing as true objectivity. Teachers still have to use their professional judgment to determine which method of calculation to use, which assignments count more than others, what goes into each assignment, and whether improvement matters.

Permitting Rewrites

One easy way to use the most recent evidence of learning is to allow students to rewrite and redo assignments, quizzes, and tests. If implemented effectively, rewrites offer students a second chance to demonstrate how much they know in relation to the intended learning.

One argument brought up against the use of rewrites is that the real world doesn't allow the equivalent of rewrites. This notion brings us back to a quotation first presented in Chapter 2: *"I'm sorry, Kevin, your second driving test is excellent, but when I average it from your first test, you still fail."* You would never hear this in the real world. The real world is full of do-over opportunities. Whether it is a driving test, a cholesterol test, or even the legal system, the *one-and-done* approach is rarely in effect, whereas second chances are prevalent.

Granted, preparing a rewrite is an easier task in some subject areas than in others. For example, it is fairly easy to create a re-test for math since only the numbers need to change to create different questions. For other subjects such as social studies, a re-test might be a little more challenging to create; however, there may be less need to create a new test. It is possible for students to take the same test if it involves extended written responses or a different form of response (e.g., oral responses instead of written). If, however, teachers want to support students with multiple opportunities to demonstrate their learning, they will find the time to make the rewrites possible. No matter what the subject area, I eventually grew to a point where *learning* was my only priority, and all students had an opportunity rewrite anything if they felt they had improved.

When I taught math, for example, all of my students had the opportunity to rewrite their tests. Students could also redo their practice assignments; however, those assignments didn't feel like rewrites because practice didn't count. I never had students rewrite quizzes because as the curriculum built upon itself, I knew, there would be future opportunities to demonstrate growth and factor improvement into their grades. If students outperformed themselves on major assignments, quizzes, or tests, I didn't count the previous assignments anyway.

As I became more focused on learning and less focused on tasks, rewrites no longer felt like second chances. Rather, they felt like natural occurrences designed for me to learn where my students were on their learning continuum. In light of all we know about test-taking environments, test anxiety, differentiation, and developmental learning, it seems unrealistic that every student will be ready for a test on the exact same day. That said, the curriculum does have to be covered, so I felt it was important to give students at least one more attempt to demonstrate their learning.

There is a catch to the rewrite opportunity, however; teachers often worry that some students will take advantage of the system. The most prominent myth about allowing rewrites is that students will disregard the first test because they know they can do a rewrite. While that might be true for some individuals, most students greatly appreciate the opportunity for a second chance. Obviously, this issue is something teachers have to pay attention to.

If a student consistently shows that he or she is not taking the first test seriously, it may be that the individual needs a special or specific routine for rewrites and redos. This problem is difficult to determine, however. How do we know whether the poor results stem from a lack of preparation and effort, or a lack of readiness? Given the way students try to guard their emotions around poor results, how do we measure whether a student has taken a test seriously? Once teachers know the students, determining this becomes easier, but never easy. The key here is to pay attention to the results and look for anomalies in student performance that might signal a student has not prepared thoroughly for the test. Even that is difficult to determine, however, since life challenges may affect how students perform, and students aren't always forthright in identifying them for their teachers.

I always told my students that they had to *redo* or *relearn* before they could *rewrite*. There has to be some new learning, some new thinking, or some new routines developed before the rewrite is given. Figure 9.3 (see next page) shows an example of what a typical week would look like after a unit test in one of my classes. The question of what to do with the two scores is always prominent. I used the higher of the two scores, as it is possible for the second test to be lower than the first. Disruptions at home, issues with friends, or life circumstances—all reasons why students perform poorly on tests—are as likely to happen on re-test day as on the day of the original test. Averaging the two, as discussed earlier, limits our ability to truly reflect student progress and improvement. By discounting (on most occasions) the original test score, the original test becomes a formative tool that directs future learning.

It is difficult for teachers to keep formative and summative assessments completely separate throughout their practice. What's more realistic is to find a way to balance the two and allow them to play a natural, fluid role in the teaching and learning process. One important aspect of formative assessments is that they do not play a role in determining report card grades designed to report to others about student progress. By eliminating the original test from the calculation of the grade, a more productive balance is struck.

> Some have argued that formative and summative assessments are so different in their purpose that they must be kept apart... However, it is unrealistic to expect teachers and students to practice such separation, so the challenge is to achieve a more positive relationship between the two. (Black, et al., 2004, p. 15)

Dropping the original or lowest score seems to put students at ease. They know they have the opportunity to recover from the result of the original test. This practice is one way to better factor student improvement into the grading and reporting process.

Figure 9.3: Weekly Schedule After a Unit Test

MONDAY: I return the original test to the students. As a class, we go over each test question to identify the correct process and answer. Students then complete their test review and learning plan (see Chapter 6). I collect those plans at the end of the class. After school, I prepare learning packages for students to use for additional learning.

TUESDAY, WEDNESDAY, THURSDAY: Typically, these three days are spent reteaching and relearning. I spend my time with small groups, working on specific sections of the test that they found challenging. Working with this small group, I identify student-specific challenges and help prevent the students from making the same mistakes again. The other students work independently until it is their time to work with me on their concerns. Students who score very high (or perfect) on the original test are given topics and questions that are beyond their grade level to stretch their thinking. These, of course, don't count, but provide them with a further challenge.

FRIDAY: All students rewrite the test, even the students who first scored extremely high. I ask those students to rewrite to validate the results of the test. They are my control group. If they score poorly on the second test, it might indicate to me that the re-test was too difficult in comparison with the first test. I have never had a student refuse to write a test under these conditions.

Emphasizing Most Recent Evidence of Learning

On a larger scale, students can change (improve) tremendously over the course of a year or even a semester. Using the most recent evidence of learning allows for individual differences in how students process and demonstrate their learning. When focused on learning, teachers more readily understand the need for grades to reflect where a student is, as opposed to where he or she was. What happened *before* should not limit the grade's ability to truly reflect the student's improved status.

> It is much better to simply use the more recent information; students then get full credit for their improvement rather than a score based on artificial manipulation of numbers. We are able to focus on grading as an exercise in professional judgment, rather than as an exercise in mechanical number crunching.

> Improvement is best considered as a reporting variable and not primarily a grading variable. Grades then are based on the students' most consistent level of achievement, with special consideration for more recent achievement. (O'Connor, 2002, pp. 128–129)

Improvement renders previous evidence of learning irrelevant. Once a student has moved past a previous level of progress, the previous level of progress is no longer a reflection of where the student is in his or her learning. When we emphasize the recent learning evidence, either within specific units of study or throughout the entire semester, both student and parents have a clearer picture of what the student has achieved.

Chris Terris, a high-school English teacher at Penticton Secondary School, began his assessment and grading journey as a healthy skeptic; however, he has seen the impact that sound assessment and grading have had in his classroom. Chris is convinced we need to challenge the way grading has always been done in terms of what we know is right and how our students respond.

To say I was initially resistant to making significant changes to my grading practices would be an understatement. Groomed at "Dinosaur College," I was adamant that any policy change that softened the expectations on students or made me, as the teacher, more responsible for students' success and made them less responsible was not going to occur within my four walls. It stemmed from a misguided interpretation: grading practices were being modified to lower standards. It wasn't enough that graduation standards had been hijacked; now the mandate was coming to change daily grading practices, making it all but impossible for any student with a pulse not to graduate and feel good about his "accomplishments."

Change occurred slowly. I attended a few sessions on grading practices, agreed to take part in a district initiative looking at assessment, and engaged in a few moments of personal reflection (it didn't hurt that I had two teenagers at home whose teachers were all over the board regarding their assessment). There were

■ ■ ■

a few hurdles to overcome. If any changes were to occur, I was going to make sure that they did not involve lower standards of assessment or lessen student responsibility.

I slowly began to make several changes to my classroom practices. Among many of the changes I made (no late penalties, re-tests, etc.) was the implementation of "weighted assessments." In cases of repetitive skill assessment, the best results are often weighted more heavily. For example, if we are working on writing effective responses to literature during a novel unit, students may have two or three opportunities to demonstrate their ability. A lower result may be omitted or weighted less in order for students to demonstrate improvement. What was interesting is how overwhelmingly supportive the students themselves were of this change. Here's what a few of my students told me:

"This gives a boost to students' self-esteem and rewards the development of skills."

"It is a fair assessment because the goal of a teacher is to have students grow and rewarding them [for this growth] is right."

"The feedback after the first set is great. Also, heavier weighting pressures students to accomplish more than the first time."

I also conducted a more thorough survey/reflection with my students to gauge how they felt about the grading practices I had implemented. When surveyed, 93 percent of my students agreed that the new grading practices were fairer and give students a better chance to show what they know; students' marks will be a more accurate reflection of their understanding. Even the other 7 percent admitted the practices were fairer; their question was whether the changes as a whole might support poor work habits. More student responses:

"Grading should only be about the students' abilities. There should be consequences for the work habits, but the grade should show the student's ability."

"The grading practices encourage students to always do the best that they can do even if it takes longer than others. You can't rush perfection."

"These grading practices do give students better opportunities to show their best potential. The marks taken off such as late marks have nothing to do with student's knowledge of the subject."

Along with my classroom responsibilities, I have been coaching basketball for 23 years. As a coach, I am very sensitive to putting my players in positions to be successful both individually and collectively. Assessment of players occurs during practice, but especially during game situations—pressure tests if you like. It's my job to make sure that individual players have an opportunity to enter a situation where they can have success. Obviously, not all players are equal to all situations. When scheduling games, I consider the strength of my own team, hoping to challenge them but not put them in a situation to be embarrassed or that might shatter their confidence.

During this process, a few questions came to mind: Was I doing the same in the classroom? If not, why not, if I believe in my coaching philosophy? When confident, my players and team are always more successful. Shouldn't my grading practices be designed to help students build on success? As a coach, I attack every season with the end in mind—the end of the season, the next season for my players, and their eventual enjoyment of the game without my guidance. I strongly believe that the changes made in my grading practices better reflect this philosophy. I now attack my courses with the same mentality: I am building for the end of the year (maybe a provincial exam), the following year for my students, and, ultimately, for the time when my students move on without me. When my players leave me, I hope that I have instilled in them a love of the game so that they continue to be involved at some level. When my students leave me, I hope that I have instilled a love of learning and, specifically, a love of literature.

Chris's story shows that when we take that first step to try something new, make learning the priority, and reflect with the students to confirm that what has changed is in the students' best interest, even the most healthy skeptic will never return to the way grading has always been done. The benefits to both teachers and students are overwhelming.

Tips for Communicating with Parents

- By relying solely on mathematical precision, we risk undermining parents' confidence in our ability to use professional judgment to recognize learning and improvement. As students go through a year, parents recognize their child's improvement as much as we do. Most parents believe that improvement should count for something. Parents want us to go *beyond the numbers* and look at significant improvement their child has made.

- Communicate to parents *how* improvement will factor into their child's grade. The mathematical calculation of grades, especially when the weighting of task types is involved, can be confusing. As you implement an *improvement* mindset, let parents know
  - how you balance both past and current levels of performance
  - how you re-test
  - how a student does a rewrite
  - how you will account for outlier performances that stray far from the norm

Guiding Questions for Individuals or Learning Teams

1. What role does improvement currently play within your grading practices?

2. Recognizing that all three measures of central tendency have pros and cons and that using the *mean* score is the most widely used calculation, describe your experiences with using the *median* or *mode* score to determine students' grades.

3. Is it fair that students who know and understand the core learning of a course before taking it receive high grades on their report cards? Why or why not?

4. Why are some teachers reluctant to allow students to rewrite or redo assignments, quizzes, or tests? What measures could be put in place to control for these concerns? What is your position or policy on rewrites?

5. Why is the *most recent evidence* more accurate than measures of central tendency when it comes to student grades? What challenges might you anticipate when emphasizing the most recent evidence? How would you try to control for those challenges?

Chapter 10

Professional Learning Matters

> *Educators must stop working in isolation and hoarding their ideas, materials, and strategies and begin to work together to meet the needs of all students.*
>
> **Richard DuFour**

Teaching can be a lonely profession; it is often done in isolation and rarely performed with a team. Teachers can spend their entire career never truly working with other teachers in their school. Being employed in the same building does not necessarily lead to teamwork, collaboration, or interdependency. Likewise, even teachers in the same school who teach the same subjects or grades may never take (or been given) the opportunity to work together. Isolation is, as Mike Schmoker (2005) points out, the enemy of improvement and can lead teachers to a point where they are no longer connected to what is relevant for today's classrooms.

Still others, even if they choose to work alone, might never take the opportunity to keep learning to improve their craft. While most schools' mission statements likely refer to developing students as *lifelong learners*, adults within a school committed to this mission may not develop as lifelong learners themselves. As we begin to implement new assessment for learning strategies and sound grading practices, taking the time to learn, reflect, and grow is even more critical to the sustainability of what is being implemented. Without this professional learning, we run the risk of eventually being out of touch and irrelevant within the context of our own work.

Big Idea: Professional Learning for the Sake of Student Achievement

It is our professional responsibility to remain current with the latest findings about how to best serve our students. There are countless examples of professions where not being current could have devastating results. The lawyer who is not familiar with current case law or the doctor not up to speed on the latest techniques, side effects, or trends in diagnostics would have relatively short careers. For teachers, the results of not staying current may not be as acute, but they are no less devastating. While the results of a poor surgery are likely obvious, the results of not teaching students in a way that maximizes their chances of success may not be seen until much later.

What is the total cost to an individual and society when a student does not learn to read to the level of expectation, for example? Students have the ability to cope and adjust, but this ability can't completely compensate for dated techniques, limited knowledge, and finite experience. Some student success is not always the direct result of what the teacher has done. Early in my teaching career, some students succeeded *despite* my limited skills and experience as a teacher. That said, the quality of the teacher makes the single biggest difference to the achievement results of the students taught. As a result, the achievement students gain through poor instructional quality is, at best, limited. As a former football coach of mine told me, "If *better* is possible, then *good* is not good enough!"

Education does not occur in a vacuum. As much as we continue to learn about the advancements in many other areas of life, so too have we learned in education. For example, pedagogically, we know much more about the brain, learning styles, literacy improvement, and metacognition. Being current so that we remain effective at teaching all students may now be more important than ever.

In some ways, the rate of change has been so rapid that teachers often face a never-ending parade of new initiatives. This situation can be intimidating, leading some teachers to step back to isolation as a form of mental protection. Having said that, we can't use this as an excuse for not learning and growing. Professional learning is the cornerstone of effective assessment, instruction, and grading.

As we grow, we gain experience; with experience comes wisdom. Some teachers retire with 30 years of experience; others retire with one year of experience repeated 30 times! Which teacher are you more likely to be?

Taking Part in a Professional Learning Community

While an individual teacher continuing to learn professionally is effective, it does not solve the issue of working in isolation. The loneliness of teaching can be mitigated when teachers come together as a professional learning community (PLC) to improve their practice. Working as a team, a PLC aims to improve individual practice and overall school performance through an increase in student achievement. PLCs achieve this goal by focusing on

- a shared purpose

- mutual regard and caring

- an insistence on integrity and truthfulness (Hord, 2009)

As Carol Ann Tomlinson is to differentiated instruction, Richard DuFour is to professional learning communities. While the term *PLC* can be used in a variety of ways, DuFour (2004) identified three ideas that serve as the core principles to guide schools as their learning communities develop and grow. The clarification has been necessary. As the PLC movement for school reform and improvement grew, it seemed as though any gathering of teachers was called a "learning community." Consequently, PLCs from one school to the next appeared more different than similar. While uniformity of format and process is not critical to a PLC's success, DuFour's three big ideas help keep teachers focused on the purpose of their PLC and the reason they gather. According to DuFour, PLCs have a greater chance of succeeding if they

- ensure that students learn

- develop a culture of collaboration

- focus on results

Ensure That Students Learn

Throughout this book we have discussed the notion that *learning outcomes* and *targets* are most important. Put another way, what students *learn* is far more important than ensuring that students have the opportunity to be taught. Students have to be at the centre of the education experience. Once the focus is on learning and not teaching, schools begin to explore new and various options for every student. Most schools have a mission statement that speaks of *learning for all*, but when we simply ensure that students are taught, our systems convey a collective vision of *learning for most*. If we truly mean *all*, then schools need to ask themselves some difficult questions that they may not be equipped to answer yet. Through a PLC, however, these questions can be answered and new systems and practices can be put in place. These critical questions can drive the purpose of the PLC and focus the school on learning for all. According to DuFour, every school should ask these questions:

1. What are students expected to learn or know?

2. How do we respond when they don't learn?

3. What do we do when long-term success is in jeopardy?

4. How do we individualize learning for the students who need it?

From these four overarching questions comes the development of systems, structures, and routines that improve all students' chances for success.

Teachers are busy. By focusing the conversations on learning, PLCs can feel confident that their collective time is being spent wisely and is focused on the most important job at hand. True PLCs pay attention to areas where students are having limited success, set priorities, and define one area of focus. The work will always be the work (Hord, 2009); that is, there will always be a curriculum to cover, learning outcomes to assess, feedback to be given, and final grades to produce, but PLCs are driven by a collective passion to know *more*, to understand *why*, and to determine *how*.

Develop a Culture of Collaboration

The implementation of anything new doesn't just happen. Only through professional learning will a teacher understand *what* to do, and only through a PLC can a teacher work with others on *how*—the implementation, analysis, and adjustment of these new routines focused on success for all. To implement something in isolation can be an intimidating venture, as teachers question whether they are interpreting the research correctly, thinking of all possible roadblocks and struggles, and making the correct adjustments along the way. To implement as a team via a PLC is to have all of the support needed to implement new ideas in the most effective manner. Ensuring that students learn is accomplished most effectively through the PLC model. As Rosenholtz (1989) points out, the most important effect of teacher collaboration is its impact on the uncertainty of the job, which, when faced alone, can otherwise undermine a teacher's sense of confidence. Confidence, then, is not only critical for students, but for teachers as well.

Most of us are collegial with our colleagues. We get along with one another, socialize effectively (at least at work), and manage to create a generally positive working environment. Collegiality, however, is not collaboration. Little (1990) argues that *joint* work is the strongest form of collaboration, and that if collaboration is limited to anecdotes, help given only when asked, or to pooling of existing ideas without examining and extending them, it will simply confirm the status quo. Joint work, she adds, implies and creates stronger interdependence, shared responsibility, a collective commitment and improvement, and greater readiness to take part in the collaborative work. The interdependency Little speaks of is one of need; each member of the PLC *needs* the other members to work as a team to maximize the learning process for all who are involved.

We all have to pay close attention to this interdependency, regardless of age or experience, so we do not communicate to others that we have nothing more to learn. For some, the idea of learning something from a colleague, especially one who is less experienced, can be difficult to accept. Some worry about an underlying message of weakness, or at least a lack of competence, if they don't have all of the answers. We know, however, that admitting we don't know takes strength and confidence in our ability. Once teachers can get past the stigma, most find the collaborative process professionally rewarding. This process can only benefit the students and their levels of success:

> The powerful collaboration that characterizes professional learning communities is a systematic process in which teachers work together to analyze and improve their classroom practice. Teachers work in teams, engaging in an ongoing cycle of questions that promote deep team learning. This process, in turn, leads to higher levels of student achievement. (DuFour, 2004)

Teams are comprised of *teammates* who need one another. To use a sports analogy, the difference between a golfer and a football player is that the golfer can win on his or her own merit. Playing an individual sport, the golfer doesn't need the help of any teammates to succeed. A football player, no matter how great, doesn't win without teammates.

If we all taught in one-room schoolhouses, then maybe collaboration would be overrated, although it would likely still allow a teacher to reach levels of effectiveness not possible as an individual. The vast majority of us, however, work in schools with colleagues, who often teach the same students and subjects as we do. Being part of a team can be more rewarding, as the success can be shared among the group.

While developing an effective PLC will not earn teachers any trophies, fame, or fortune, they can make an important and valuable contribution to society through the impending success of the students. Just as a group of determined and focused players will find a way to succeed, teachers can also be equally determined. Nothing happens without desire. If teachers have the desire to collaborate, they will find a rich, professional learning environment that raises their level of effectiveness, while supporting other teachers in their parallel journey toward proficiency.

Focus on Results

The third principle DuFour identified is a focus on results. Improving student achievement is the ultimate goal. A PLC's effectiveness is measured not by the number of meetings, activities, or debates that have occurred. A PLC is effective only if student achievement improves. PLCs need to centre on improving student performance. While certain programs might maximize the success of students, the implementation of these programs is the *means*, not the end.

We don't implement sound grading practices to say we've implemented them; we implement them to improve the students' chances of success. Likewise, we shouldn't implement anything until we have identified a need. If what we are doing in the classroom has students maximizing success and feeling confident and excited about future learning, then we should carry on. We should implement new programs, new processes and routines, and new ideas only when the results show that improved performance is possible, and that what is being implemented will likely produce the desired result.

This is where continual assessment *for* learning is critical— not assessment events, but the day-to-day assessments that we use to determine whether students are succeeding or not. Reflection on the results allows us to focus on areas of concern and potential solutions that move students forward. When there are occasions of common formative assessments, PLCs can work to analyze the results and determine the next steps of instruction. PLCs can look at overall achievement levels at the end of a term or semester and focus on what to improve next time. The point is that the results of our efforts need to be the ultimate guide as to whether we are succeeding. If the results are not at the expected levels, PLCs can work toward the necessary changes, improvement, and growth required to reach those anticipated levels.

Putting It into Practice

Teachers are responsible for engaging in personal professional growth and will have maximum success as part of a professional learning community.

As much as we have to learn, we can't learn it all. If PLCs are not commonplace in an individual school, all teachers need to do is take an interest in going deeper in one particular area of their profession that they feel needs some attention. The most effective way for teachers to do this is through self-directed personal inquiry that focuses on asking a question relevant to their practice, and then seeking, through an action-research model, an answer. While these inquiry-based questions can come in many forms, the most effective learning is accomplished when we seek an answer to the question *why?* Most of the empirical research is or has been done for us, which means we know what the research is telling us about reading instruction, behavioural support, formative assessment, and so on. What we may not know is what that research looks like in practice and why it makes such a difference to the success of the students.

Exploring Personal Inquiry Questions

We know from Black and Wiliam and other assessment and grading experts that descriptive feedback makes a significant difference to students' success levels. We might know this from the research, but a teacher may have never used descriptive feedback in any significant way. Therefore, a teacher may ask, "Why does descriptive feedback have a positive impact on student writing?" The teacher would then embark on a journey to learn what effective descriptive feedback looks like, when to use it, how students would use it, what is effective, what is ineffective, and so on. While the teacher is still teaching the curriculum, the inquiry-based professional learning is driven from his or her passion and professional curiosity—what the teacher still doesn't fully understand or wonders about teaching.

Continual growth and improvement is the mark of a successful person. With so much to learn, taking an in-depth look at specific topics of relevance might be the most effective, efficient, and relevant means of accomplishing this. To maintain their focus, teachers should choose a topic or a question that is of high interest and connected to their current work. Teachers should focus on real issues in real classrooms requiring real solutions or a real answer, which leads seamlessly to the action-research model. In any event, teachers who continue to professionally learn maximize the success chances for their students and keep their careers relevant and meaningful. The most significant factor in whether students learn is teaching quality, which is improved through continuous professional learning (Hord, 2009).

Establishing the PLC Context

For a PLC to thrive, every school needs contextual features to optimize success:

- School leadership that values a collaborative culture needs to be in place.

- Teachers need to be given both the time and space to conduct their PLC activities. While the time may not always be available during the instructional day, as release time can be very costly for both schools and school districts, there is a balance between professional time and volunteer time. Professional learning isn't as much an event as an ongoing process. It will occur outside the structured PLC time; however, making the time within the workday creates the balance and sends the right message that professional learning is important. Having said that, the most effective PLCs I've experienced were ones driven by a common passion for deep learning, regardless of when the learning occurred.

- PLCs need access to data. If none is available, then the PLC may have to create a new system around data collection to measure the effectiveness of its efforts. Without becoming too clinical, it is important to know whether or not the effort, practices, and new ideas are truly making a difference for student achievement. Relevant information that can assist a PLC in analyzing the impact of its work allows for an efficient and effective implementation and ongoing monitoring of the successes and challenges.

Committing to Continuous Improvement

Although all of these structural aspects need to be in place, the most important aspect is every individual's commitment to ongoing analysis, implementation, and reflection. To stay on course, PLCs need to focus their daily activities on those things that, as Dennis Sparks puts it, change the brains of teachers and administrators:

> The final two percent (of activities) is that cluster of experiences that literally change the brains of teachers and administrators. Educators have these experiences when they read, write, observe, use various thinking strategies, listen, speak, and practice new behaviors in ways that deepen understanding, affect beliefs, produce new habits of the mind and behavior, and are combined in ways that alter practice. Such professional learning produces complex, intelligent behavior in all teachers and leaders and continuously enhances their professional judgment. (Sparks, 2005 p. 161)

The continuous improvement model of a PLC, where everyone is simultaneously a learner and a teacher, has the greatest potential to improve teacher practice. The emphasis needs to be on what we do *daily* as teachers. For example, we should each ask ourselves:

- How do I learn?

- What improves achievement?

- How do I respond when learning is impeded?

- What was I thinking when I decided to teach that way?

- What are my colleagues doing that I could adopt and adapt?

These are just a few of the questions that we need to answer as we continue on our professional learning journey.

Professional learning has been a priority in all of the schools in which I have worked. The model was not one of declaring that PLCs would be implemented. Rather, our professional learning experiences were more organic; they grew from an identified need and brought together like-minded individuals who were interested in exploring the issue deeper. As the research around PLCs continued to emerge throughout the last decade, our PLC experiences continued to be refined. Whether it was the Academic Team at McNicoll Park Middle School, the School Climate Team at Princess Margaret Secondary School, or the Assessment and Grading Team at Penticton Secondary School, our goals were to improve the achievement opportunities for all of our students. Although at times we weren't fully aware of it, we were driven by DuFour's questions (see page 153), which kept us focused on what was truly important.

Driven by Overarching Questions

The four questions DuFour identified as critical for ensuring that students learn are relevant from an assessment and grading perspective, as well. Clear learning targets, expressed in student-friendly language and making note of the underpinnings, identify what students are expected to know. When students don't learn, we need to focus on differentiation, descriptive feedback, and more opportunities to practise; we also need to provide multiple opportunities to demonstrate learning, all the while focusing on the most recent evidence. When long-term success is in jeopardy, we need to

- build student confidence through relationships and support

- reconnect students to their own learning by involving them along the way

- focus on the small steps of improvement that build up to the desired outcome

- account for only the most recent evidence wherever possible

- develop new routines for students who require an individualized learning plan

The questions are universally applicable to any specific aspect of teaching and learning. Using these questions to guide our PLC activities, or even our own individual professional learning, will allow us all to be more effective with our students.

Assessment for learning and sound grading practices will allow us to teach with greater precision and report with more accuracy. To develop fluency and capacity with those practices in the most efficient and effective way, teachers should turn to the PLC model. Developing proficiency with any new idea takes time and goes through various stages of success and failure. Without a PLC, teachers might be prone to give up and go back to old habits. With the support of their PLC, teachers will be able to push through the implementation challenges and make the new ideas a part of their typical routines.

Tips for Communicating with Parents

- In both obvious and subtle ways, communicate with parents that you are continuing to learn.

- Let parents know what you are working on, what you are still curious about, or what you need to know. This sharing will, in a sense, humanize the teacher–parent relationship and allow parents to see that you are serious about the work of becoming the best teacher you can be.

- Don't make too many changes too quickly. Parents will respect the fact that you are intent on improving yourself as a professional, but they may be uncomfortable if too much changes too dramatically over a short time.

Guiding Questions for Individuals or Learning Teams

1. As a professional, what have you learned about teaching and learning in the last six months?

2. What have been your professional learning routines over the course of your career? What has been most effective? What aspects of your professional learning habits need greater attention?

3. What are (or do you anticipate will be) the most rewarding aspects of working within a PLC model?

4. Describe a time when a professional learning experience went astray or when a PLC was ineffective. What specific elements can you point to that explain why the experience was poor or why the process failed?

5. The three big ideas that DuFour identifies as core principles that should guide schools and their PLCs seem straightforward and obvious. How is it that we lose our focus from these core principles and to what do we give too much of our attention?

6. What is the *biggest idea* you will take away from this book? How do you anticipate it will make you a more effective teacher?

Andrade, H. (2007–2008). Self-assessment through rubrics. *Educational Leadership, 65*(4), 60–63.

Arter, J., & McTighe, J. (2001). *Scoring rubrics in the classroom: Using performance criteria for assessing and improving student performance.* Thousand Oaks, CA: Corwin Press.

Askew, S. (Ed.). (2000). *Feedback for learning.* New York, NY: Routledge-Falmer.

Bailey, J. M., & Guskey, T. R. (2000). *Implementing student-led conferences.* Thousand Oaks, CA: Corwin Press.

Black, P., & Wiliam, D. (1998). Inside the black box: Raising standards through classroom assessment. *Phi Delta Kappan, 80*(2), 139–148.

Black, P., Harrison, C., Lee, C., Marshall, B., & Wiliam, D. (2004). Working inside the black box: Assessment for learning in the classroom. *Phi Delta Kappan, 86*(1), 9–21.

Brodie, R. (1996). *Virus of the mind: The new science of the meme.* Carlsbad, CA: Hay House.

Brookhart, S. (2008). *How to give effective feedback to your students.* Alexandria, VA: Association for Supervision and Curriculum Development (ASCD).

Butler, R. (1988). Enhancing and undermining intrinsic motivation. *British Journal of Educational Psychology, 58,* 1–14.

Chan, E. (2001). Improving student performance by reducing anxiety. *Positive Pedagogy: Successful and Innovative Strategies in Higher Education, 1*(3). Retrieved from http://www.mcmaster.ca/cll/posped/pastissues/volume.1.no.3/reducing.anxiety.htm

Chappuis, J. (2009). *Seven strategies of assessment for learning.* Portland, OR: ETS Assessment Training Institute.

Chappuis, S., & Chappuis, J. (2007–2008). The best value in formative assessment. *Educational Leadership, 65*(4), 14–18.

Chappuis, S., & Stiggins, R. J. (2002). Classroom assessment for learning. *Educational Leadership, 60*(1), 40–44.

Covey, S. R. (1989). *The 7 habits of highly successful people.* New York, NY: Free Press.

Davies, A. (2000). *Making classroom assessment work.* Courtenay, BC: Connections Publishing.

Davies, A. (2003). Involving students in communicating about their learning. Retrieved from http://annedavies.com/images/PDFs/involving_students.pdf. Originally published in *NASSP Bulletin, 85*(621), 47–52.

Davies, A., Herbst, S., & Parrott Reynolds, B. (2008). *Transforming barriers to assessment for learning: Lessons learned from leaders.* Courtenay, BC: Connections Publishing.

DuFour, R. (2004). What is a "professional learning community"? Retrieved from http://pdonline.ascd.org/pd_online/secondary_reading/el200405_dufour.html. Originally published in *Educational Leadership, 61*(8), 6–11.

Fullan, M. (2001). *Leading in a culture of change.* San Francisco, CA: Jossey-Bass.

Fullan, M. (Ed.). (2009). *The challenge of change: Start school improvement now!* Thousand Oaks, CA: Corwin Press.

Gladwell, M. (2008). *Outliers: The story of success.* New York, NY: Little, Brown and Company.

Guskey, T. R. (2002). Computerized gradebooks and the myth of objectivity. *Phi Delta Kappan, 83*(10), 775–780.

Guskey, T. R. (2004). 0 alternatives. *Principal Leadership, 5*(2), 49–53.

Hargreaves, A., & Fullan, M. (Eds.). (2009). *Change wars.* Bloomington, IN: Solution Tree.

Hattie, J., & Timperley, H. (2007). The power of feedback. *Review of Educational Research, 77*(1), 81–112.

Hawkins, D. (1995). *Power vs force: The hidden determinants of human behavior.* West Sedona, AZ: Veritas Publishing.

Hord, S. (2009). Professional learning communities: Educators work together toward a shared purpose. *National Staff Development Council, 30*(1), 40–43.

Hume, K. (2007). *Start where they are: Differentiating for success with the young adolescent.* Toronto, ON: Pearson Canada Inc.

Jackson, R. R. (2009). *Never work harder than your students & other principles of great teaching.* Alexandria, VA: Association for Supervision & Curriculum Development (ASCD).

Kagan, S. (1992). *Cooperative learning.* San Juan Capistrano, CA: Resources for Teachers.

Kanter, R. M. (2004). *Confidence: How winning streaks & losing streaks begin and end.* New York, NY: Crown Business.

Little, J. W. (1990). The persistence of privacy: Autonomy and initiative in teachers' professional relations. *Teachers College Record, 91*(4), 509–536.

Marzano, R. J. (2007). *The art & science of teaching.* Alexandria, VA: Association for Supervision & Curriculum Development (ASCD).

McTighe, J., & O'Connor, K. (2005). Seven practices for effective learning. *Educational Leadership, 63*(3), 10–17.

Morreale, C. (March 2000). Leadership for gifted education, IAGC graduate course, Northwestern University, Evanston, IL.

O'Connor, K. (2002). *How to grade for learning: Linking grades to standards* (2nd ed.). Thousand Oaks, CA: Corwin Press.

O'Connor, K. (2007). *A repair kit for grading: 15 fixes for broken grades.* Portland, OR: ETS Assessment Training Institute.

Popham, W. J. (2008). *Transformative assessment.* Alexandria, VA: Association for Supervision and Curriculum Development (ASCD).

Reeves, D. (2007). *Ahead of the curve: The power of assessment to transform teaching and learning.* Bloomington, IN: Solution Tree.

Reeves, D. (2010). *Elements of grading: A guide to effective practice.* Bloomington, IN: Solution Tree.

Rosenholtz, S. (1989). *Teachers' workplace: The social organization of schools.* New York, NY: Longman.

Schmoker, M. (2005). No turning back: The ironclad case for professional learning communities. In R. DuFour et al. (Eds.), *On common ground: The power of professional learning communities* (pp. 135–153). National Education Service.

Sparks, D. (2005). Leading for transformation in teaching, learning, and relationships. In R. DuFour et al. (Eds.), *On common ground: The power of professional learning communities* (pp. 155–175). National Education Service.

Stiggins, R. (2004). New assessment beliefs from a new school mission. *Phi Delta Kappan, 86*(1), 22–27.

Stiggins, R (2008). *Assessment manifesto: A call for the development of balanced assessment systems.* Portland, OR: ETS Assessment Training Institute.

Stiggins, R., Arter, J., Chappuis, J., & Chappuis, S. (2009). *Classroom assessment for student learning: Doing it right—Using it well.* New York, NY: Allyn & Bacon.

Sullo, B. (2007). *Activating the desire to learn.* Alexandria, VA: Association for Supervision and Curriculum Development (ASCD).

Tomlinson, C. A. (2003). Deciding to teach them all. *Educational Leadership, 61*(2), 45–49.

Tomlinson, C. A. (2008). The goals of differentiation. *Educational Leadership, 66*(3), 26–30.

Tomlinson, C. A., Brimijoin, K., & Narvaez, L. (2008). *The differentiated school: Making revolutionary changes in teaching and learning.* Alexandria, VA: Association for Supervision and Curriculum Development (ASCD).

Tomlinson, C. A., & Imbeau, M. B. (2010). *Leading and managing a differentiated classroom.* Alexandria, VA: Association for Supervision and Curriculum Development (ASCD).

Vatterott, C. (2009). *Rethinking homework: Best practices that support diverse needs.* Alexandria, VA: ASCD.

Vokoun, M. J., & Bigelow, T. P. Dude, what choice do I have? *Educational Leadership, 63*(3), 70–74.

Wiggins, G. (1998). *Educative assessment: Designing assessments to inform and improve student performance.* San Francisco, CA: Jossey-Bass.

Winger, T. (2005). Grading to communicate. *Educational Leadership, 63*(3), 61–65.

Wormeli, R. (2007). *Differentiation: From planning to practice, grades 6–12.* Portland, ME: Stenhouse Publishers.

Index

communities, 152–156, 157, 158–161
and culture of collaboration, 154–156
and focus on results, 156
personal inquiry questions, 157–158
and student achievement, 151–152

R
Readiness
    assessment of, 44–45
    for evaluation, 18
    for feedback, 56–57
Reasoning targets
    defined, 35
    multiple-choice questions and, 37
    in student-friendly language, 40, 41
Research
    on best practice, 2
    currency with, 6, 18, 151
    on feedback, 49
    in formative assessment, 32
    keeping up with, 2
    on student ownership, 84
Review of work by students, 94
Rewrites, 141–144
Rosenholtz, S., 154
Rubrics
    co-construction with students, 60
    converting scores to grades, 115–117
    and descriptive feedback, 57–60
    and performance targets, 59–60

and product learning targets, 59–60
student-friendly, 51, 52
Russill, Cindy, 25–27

S
Schmoker, Mike, 150
School year, start of, 17
Scope-and-sequence paradigm, 64, 65, 135
Searcy, Naryn, 76–77
Self-assessment
    assessment accuracy and, 45
    and confidence, 43
    and descriptive feedback, 61, 85–86
    as formative, 87
    justification of, 87
    practice and, 128
    self-evaluation vs., 86
    and student ownership, 85–87, 91
    summative assessment and, 128
Self-reflection, 88
Short answer questions
    reasoning and, 37
    skills targets and, 38
    as traditional assessment method, 36
Skills
    assessment of, 38
    targets, 40, 41–42
Sparks, Dennis, 159
Standardized testing, 32
Stiggins, Rick, 18, 31–32
    Assessment Manifesto, 36–37
Struggling students, 24, 124–125, 126, 127